To John, best wishes
from Millvina Dean. April 2009.

Titanic

The Last Survivor

The life
of
Millvina Dean

By
Anthony Cunningham and Sheila Jemima
with Millvina Dean

RMS *Titanic* at sea in 1912. The clean lines of the vessel are shown to good effect in this photographic study.

'Have a kind heart and a sense of humour.'   **Millvina Dean, May 2008**

Published by

Waterfront

A division of Kingfisher Productions
Watershed Mill, Settle, North Yorkshire BD24 9LR
www.railwayvideo.com
October 2008

ISBN 978 0 946184 68 2

Printed by The Amadeus Press, Cleckheaton, West Yorkshire

Contents

A rare deck scene on board *Titanic*. Southampton City Museums

Introduction

In 1920, when I was eight years old, my mother decided to get remarried. I never knew my real father and lived in blissful ignorance as to what had happened to him so my mother's news didn't particularly bother me. Besides, the only father figure I had ever known or wanted was my grandfather whom I loved dearly. Since I wasn't a terribly curious child I never thought to ask what had happened to my real father. Then she told me.

The *Titanic* meant very little to me at the time. Nobody seemed to talk about it very much and the fact that my father had died on the ship didn't really make a huge impression on me. After all, what was the *Titanic* to me? It didn't seem to have any bearing on my world at all. That I had been the youngest survivor of the disaster meant even less! My mother told me the bare facts and that was that. It was something buried deep in her past and a subject that she didn't seem to want to discuss.

The *Titanic* hardly touched my life again until the wreck was discovered in the mid 'eighties. Until then, I hardly gave it a thought. Suddenly however, complete strangers wanted to interview me for television and newspapers, I was asked to sign autographs, give talks and make personal appearances. At first it was rather bewildering but it's amazing how quickly one can adapt to new experiences. Since I love meeting new people I have, by and large, thoroughly enjoyed the last twenty five years and am still continually amazed at how the *Titanic* disaster still touches people.

Anthony Cunningham and Sheila Jemima have produced an admirable book which will please anyone with an interest in my life story. Between them the authors have spent many hours chatting with me to get the facts straight. In addition, they have dug out old newspaper reports, letters, magazine articles and photographs to make this biography as accurate as possible. I do hope you enjoy it.

Millvina Dean
October, 2008

Left: **Vere and Millvina. pictured in 1919, seven years following the *Titanic* tragedy.**

Chapter One
Family background

This story begins in the West Country, England. Branscombe is a picturesque village in East Devon. It is believed to be the 'longest village in the country' with rows of quaint cottages set in a sweeping valley which curves down to the sea. Today the village relies on tourism for its lifeblood and is a most desirable location for second home owners. However, in the 1880s the main sources of revenue for the villagers were fishing, farming or skilled and unskilled labouring.

Millvina's father, Bertram Frank Dean, was born in New Castle Cottage Branscombe on Wednesday 30th June 1886. His father and mother were Solomon and Eliza Dean. Solomon was a Thatcher and his trade lives on today because many of the cottages in Branscombe still have that particular distinctive roof covering. Eliza Dean (nee Rendell) came from a long line of skilled Honiton lace makers. This was a cottage industry and women like Eliza would work from home. Honiton lace is one of the many varieties of hand-made bobbin lace produced commercially over the past few centuries, a lace that has become world famous for its intricate, delicate and very beautiful design. Eliza would have learned this trade from her own mother Sarah, who was also a lace maker.

Honiton lace has been made in the East Devon area since the late 16th Century and during that time has been purchased and worn by the wealthy of the world. Honiton was a wool and flax area, and had a history of textile production, so was ideally suited to producing this very fine lace. The lace takes its name from the East Devon town of Honiton where the majority of the lace was made in the past. Today, Honiton lace is a generic name for the techniques and designs involved in making this type of lace and does not necessarily have to be made in the town of Honiton. In fact, there are still people making Honiton lace throughout the world as a hobby.

During the early 19th century the industry was in serious decline because of the increase in machine made lace. However, production received a boost because of a rather special commission. The trimmings, flounces and veil for Queen Victoria's wedding dress, as well as lace for her morning dress, were ordered from Miss Bidney of Beer. Two Hundred lace-makers, mainly from Beer and Branscombe, were employed. The lace cost £1,000 and was 'akin in beauty to the diaphanous tracery of cobwebs couched in hoar-frost'. Queen Victoria was so pleased with the work that she sent for Jane Bidney. Jane left the village for the first time in her life and travelled by mail coach to court. She was also invited to the royal wedding.

Below: **Branscombe 1881. New Castle Cottage in background on the left.** *Courtesy of the Masons Arms*

Branscombe seen in 2008. Compare this scene with that taken in 1881 on the prevous page.

From 'The Branscombe lace-Makers' edited by Barbara Farquharson and Joan Doern 2002

Victoria was to be married to her cousin Prince Albert in February in the Chapel Royal of St James's Palace. The Queen was delighted with the veil and in 1841 she ordered more lace for the christening gown for her first born child Princess Victoria. The Royal family has used this same christening gown for all the royal children ever since, including the christenings of the heir to the throne, Prince Charles, and his son Prince William.

Eliza's income from lace making would have been an invaluable help in supporting the growing family. However, it was still poorly paid work, and the only form of education for children in Branscombe up until the late 1800's was the lace school. Here they were taught by the 'Lace Dame'. Children as young as five to seven years old would be working 12 hours a day making lace.

The Dean's first son Fred was born in 1884 and brought up amongst the hustle and bustle

of a working class family. By 1910 the family had moved from New Castle Cottage to Culver Hole in Branscombe, and as well as Fred there was Bertram aged 15, Willie 13, Millie 10, Harold eight, Charles four and the youngest child one year old Violet. One can only sympathise with Eliza trying to nurse, clothe and feed so many on limited resources.

Each child would be expected to begin working as soon as their rudimentary education was over. In order

Right: **An example of Honiton Lace.**

to help things along at home, and by the age of 15, Bertram was labouring on a local farm. This would have been a poorly paid job which involved long hours of hard physical work.

However, it was clearly not a life Bertram wanted to pursue and sometime after the turn of the century he went to London to seek his fortune like so many others before him. He settled in the Smithfield Market area of the City and may have worked in a number of jobs. However, by the end of the first decade he was working as a barman.

Bertram Dean must have been a cheerful, affable man because being a barman was a very sociable job and certainly not one for a shy, retiring person. It was a reasonably respectable position to have in Edwardian London and quite different to the backbreaking toil and hardship of farm life that he had left behind. Being a barman also afforded Bertram some leisure time. One of the common pursuits of the Edwardian era was to take walks in the well tended municipal parks, perhaps to stop and listen to a band, feed the ducks on the lake, read a book, promenade, or simply to sit and relax. It was in Dulwich Park, south of the River Thames that Bertram was to meet the lady

New Castle Cottage in 2008.

who was to become his future wife: Eva Georgette Light.

Eva (who called herself Ettie) was working 'in service' as a nursery nurse. Perhaps she had been taking her charges out for a walk in the park when she encountered the handsome Bertram with his trim gait, slicked back hair and rakish moustache. Ettie was a pretty young woman with a slim, hour glass figure and

Dulwich Park where Ettie and Bertram met for the first time.

Above: **A portrait of Millvina's mother Ettie.**

Below: **Bartley Village in the New Forest c.1900.**

long dark hair piled high in the fashionable 'cottage loaf' style of the day. They certainly made a fine looking couple. Perhaps their relationship started simply by a polite nod to each as they passed, later a smile and a word or two about the weather until the talk became more friendly and intimate. Whichever way it began, over a period of time the couple fell in love.

Perhaps Ettie could relate to Bertram's ambitions of self betterment and the desire to open out ones horizons. Was that part of their mutual attraction?

Ettie was born on Sunday 18th May 1879 the first child of George and Alice Light in the village of Bartley in the New Forest.

Ettie's father owned Bartley Farm which was over 64 acres - a considerable amount even by today's standards. In fact, George Light's ancestors had all been prosperous land owners - mostly in the timber and charcoal burning trade. Charcoal burning is one of England's oldest industries, being used in the manufacture of glassware and earthenware vessels. The trade is still practiced in the New Forest today.

George employed at least three men on the farm and so we can assume that he was a man of some means. The family also had a servant called Ellen so Alice would have been spared the worst of the disagreeable 'rough work' of running a large farmhouse.

Millvina remembers: 'The farm had cows, pigs, geese and horses. There was no electricity and water was drawn from the well. In later years the land was sold off and my Grandmother changed the name of the farmhouse to Regis.'

The Light family became larger and larger as the years rolled by and Bartley Farm must have been a

Above: **Chinham Street. Bartley. Millvina's early years were spent at Barley Farm which was owned by her grandfather.**

noisy and lively place. Alice was to be more or less continually pregnant for the next 19 years. After Ettie came Ernest, followed by Lawrence, Edith, Glen, Ernest, Nelsie, Gwendoline, Creswell, Douglas, Winifred, Francis, Freda and Gladys. However, like many families at this time, the Lights were to suffer the

agony of losing two of their children. Glen died just after his first birthday and Gwendoline succumbed to an illness after only 10 months.

Below: **Bartley Village C.1900.   *Courtesy Mr L Hickman***

From left, Bertram, Ettie and 2-year old Vere with Bertram's brother and sister Millie in Branscombe shortly before they left for America. *Courtesy of Dawn Squire*

Above: Grove Farm which was very similar to Bartley Farm where Millvina grew up. *Below :* Georgette, Millie and Nelsie.

Chapter Two
A New Life

It is clear that the country life was not broad enough for Ettie and, whatever her parents' ideas about it, she decided to go and find employment in London sometime after her 21st birthday. She eventually found work as a nursery maid for a family in Dulwich. It was a job she must have been used to because she no doubt had to look after nearly all of her younger brothers and sisters at one time or another.

One can't help thinking that it was something of a step down socially because Ettie had not come from a poor family and most likely did not need to work. But on balance, it seems that London life - even if it did mean looking after someone else's children - was a far more attractive prospect.

In 1910 Ettie and Bertram decided to name the day. Their wedding took place in Wandsworth Town Hall. Among the witnesses was Bertram's brother Frederick, who had perhaps also joined his brother in London to carve out a new life for himself.

The couple decided to move down to Southampton and took up residence at 120 Northumberland Road in the Northam area of the city. Later that year the couple had their first son Bertram (always known in the family circle as Vere). Bertram found work as a barman once more but this time at sea - possibly aboard a ship on the Isle of Wight service.

For a while it seems that the Deans were happily settled in Southampton. Then, in mid 1911 Ettie became pregnant again. Bertram now had to support his growing family on a barman's wages which can't have been easy. However, his hard work paid off because he was soon running his own pub -

1

Left: Bertram Dean, a very handsome upstanding man who ran The Coopers Arms in Peckham, South London, before deciding to take his young family to Kansas, USA to start a new life. Sadly he would never arrive in north America and the family's new plans were at an end.

Below: A street scene in Kansas where the Dean's were heading for in April 1912.

Wandsworth Town Hall, where Ettie and Bertram married.

The Cooper's Arms, on Bird in Bush Road, North Peckham. Why the Dean's came back into South London is a mystery. However, they lived over the pub and settled there for some time with Bertram running the bar and Ettie busy looking after little Vere and awaiting the birth of her next child.

It was around this time that Ettie received a letter from her uncle Alfred which would have far reaching repercussions on the entire family.

In October, 1871, Alfred Norbury had arrived in Kansas City to start a new life. Things had worked out well for him and over the years he had prospered. His letter must have painted a glowing portrait of the good life to be had there, because Bertram and Ettie made the monumental decision to emigrate. Uncle Alfred would give them a lodging in his home - a brand new limestone and brick residence built in 1911 at 3659 Harrison Street, Kansas City - until they got settled in their own place. When he got there Bertram planned to open a tobacconist shop.

However, the couple had to stall their plans for a while because there were soon more pressing events to deal with closer to home, when Ettie gave birth to her second child.

Eliza Gladys Milvina Dean was born on Friday, 2nd February, 1912 in a bedroom above The Cooper's

Bertram Dean (right) and two friends.

Arms. Somehow the baby acquired her pet name 'Millvina' perhaps, after Bertram's cousin Millie. (Milvina's birth certificate shows her name with one L but Millvina has always spelt it with two.) Ettie may also have been showing a preferential fondness for her youngest sister Gladys by using the name for her own daughter. Ettie herself registered the birth just over a month later on 13th March in Camberwell.

But even this event wasn't going to stand in the way of Bertram and Ettie's plan to leave England. Arrangements were made, possessions were sold, tickets were booked. On April 10th, 1912 the family party set off. Their adventure was about to begin.

Just before they left, they went back to Branscombe to say goodbye to Bertram's family. Lily Gush, a cousin who was 12 yrs old at the time, remembers waving them off from the upstairs window of her cottage 'Little Seaside' apparently the whole village turned out to say goodbye.

Chapter Three

Titanic

Millvina recalls: 'The odd thing about the whole story is that we weren't even supposed to go on the *Titanic* originally. We had been booked onto another ship called the *Philadelphia* but there was a coal strike at the time and so all of the coal had to be taken off the other smaller ships so that the *Titanic* could make its maiden voyage.'

The strike was settled by April 6th, but it would be some time before the newly mined coal would be shipped to Southampton to replenish the laid up steamers like White Star's *Oceanic* and *Majestic* and American line's *New York, Philadelphia, St Louis* and *St Paul*.

'The White Star Line got in touch with my father and asked him if he would like to change his booking - would he like to go on the *Titanic* instead? Well, everyone had heard of the wonderful *Titanic* and so of

the dock and he said, 'You'll have a wonderful time, it's a wonderful ship!'. In all the excitement they did not hear the call for visitors to go ashore, and nearly sailed with the *Titanic* too! My grandfather apparently was in quite a state, because he had to get back to the farm to milk the cows. He was also worried about his horse and cart left on the dockside.'

Commissioned as the largest ship in the world and fitted with innovative safety features and luxurious appointments, the *Titanic* was a fine addition to the White Star Line. Although it was never claimed by her owners, there was a popular myth spread abroad by the press that she was 'unsinkable'. She was commonly regarded as the height of luxury, speed and man's triumph over nature.

Such was this confidence in modern engineering that *Titanic*'s Captain, Edward J Smith, actually said of

Titanic **slips away from her berth at Southampton on 10th April 1912.**

course he jumped at the chance. I expect he thought he was terribly fortunate so he agreed straight away! My mother said that he was so excited about it because the *Titanic* was such a magnificent ship.'

My grandfather George Light, and my Aunt Gladys came down to see us off in his pony and trap at

the *Adriatic* – an earlier White Star liner, 'I cannot imagine any condition which would cause a ship to founder. I cannot conceive of any disaster happening to this vessel. Modern shipbuilding has gone beyond that…' *'Titanic Voices publication'*

When the *Titanic* left her builders Harland & Wolff,

Left: *Titanic* **moored in Southampton Docks on Good Friday 1912.** *Southern Daily Echo*

Belfast, and arrived in Southampton on April 4th to prepare for her maiden voyage on the 10th, there was a high demand for jobs on her because of the recent coal strike, with over 17,000 men out of work in the town. A Southampton resident recalled: 'There was no such thing as a permanent job in those days. You were in work one day and out the next, and often men were recruited in pubs by buying a drink for the boss…' [Titanic Voices]

Journalist A. Temple, writing in the 'Southampton Times' observed: 'In almost every street numbers of working men were aimlessly about idle. Men went out in the morning to look for work, pulling their belts tighter to make up for their lack of breakfast, while their children went to school cold and with their hunger only partly satisfied…'

Titanic **leaving on her maiden voyage. Crowds watch as she passes the liner** New York. **Many were unaware that the backwash from the** Titanic **broke the mooring ropes of the** New York. **A collision was prevented by Captain Gale on the tug** Vulcan.

At 12 noon on 10th April, in brilliant sunshine, the Titanic cast off with pilot George Bowyer to guide her out down Southampton Water on her maiden voyage to America, leaving behind crowds of onlookers lining the White Star Dock waving their loved ones goodbye. One can only imagine the thoughts of Millvina's Grandfather and Aunt who must have wondered if they would ever see their loved ones again.

The Titanic was carrying approximately 2, 228 passengers and crew, and at nine weeks old Millvina was the youngest passenger on board.

'My mother and father had sold nearly everything they had in order to emigrate.' said Millvina. 'We had to go steerage [Third Class] to save money but everyone said that it would be lovely because it was better than most First Class accommodation on other older ships! All in all, my parents were as happy as could be.

I can't help thinking that my mother was terribly brave. Can you imagine having to take two such small children on such a long journey into the unknown? I was only nine weeks old and Vere was just about walking! Even though she had her hands full she was just about able to send a couple of lines on a postcard to my grandmother [Alice Light] to tell her that everything was fine, but she must have been worried about what lay ahead.'

> *Dear Mother,*
> *Just a card to say we are enjoying ourselves fine up to now. Little baby was very restless. With best love, Ettie.*
> [Ken Marschall Collection]

The first port of call was at the French port of Cherbourg, where the Titanic picked up more people. Some of the passengers were dropped off, including 11 year old Eileen Lenox-Conyngham whose family were going to France on holiday: 'We were all of us very bad sailors. Mother wanted the largest, safest, steadiest ship afloat. She chose the Titanic.' [Southampton Oral History Unit]

Titanic left Cherbourg at 8.10 and arrived in Queenstown, Ireland at 11.30, picking up second and third class passengers and emigrants, as well as 1385 sacks of mail. The very last letters from crew and passengers were posted in Queenstown, many of which arrived at their destinations before news of the disaster was known.

Below and inset: Postcard from Ettie to her parents posted in Queenstown, the liner's last port of call. Note that the postcard view is actually incorrect in so far as the *Titanic* had an enclosed portion of its promenade deck which is clearly seen in the photograph above.

Chapter Four

Disaster

Four days after departing Southampton, on a calm, starlit night, the *Titanic* collided with an iceberg and sank in just over two hours. Tragically the loss of life was increased by the serious shortage of lifeboats. Only 705 people survived to complete their journey.

Millvina: 'My mother told me that we had a lovely time up until the disaster. She remembered a band that used to play jolly tunes sometimes in the saloon but not much else apart from that. It was as if she later blanked out the whole thing from her mind.

I was about eight years old when she described what happened. Up until then I had absolutely no idea that I had even been on the *Titanic*! I think that it was too awful for her to discuss and losing my father was so painful for her that my mother just wanted to forget about it. However, this is what she told me:

The *Titanic* had been at sea for a few days and everything had been fine. One night when we were all asleep in our little cabin my father woke my mother up and said, 'There's something wrong with the ship! I heard a crash!' He went up to the deck to investigate and then rushed back down and told my mother to get us all dressed in warm clothes and go and find a lifeboat because the ship had hit an iceberg! My mother carried me in her arms and I suppose my father carried Vere because he was so small too - he was only a toddler. All our money had gone to the Purser's safe but at some point my father gave my mother his silver watch for safe keeping.

My mother was about to get into a lifeboat when something awful happened. Vere toddled off! He wandered into the crowds of anxious passengers and disappeared. My father went off to find him and that was the last she saw of him. She had no idea if either of them would be alright. It was absolutely dreadful and she was sick with worry. At least she knew I was safe which must have been some kind of consolation I suppose. The problem was that at first no one thought the *Titanic* would actually sink so, nobody rushed for the boats and there was no panic. Apparently, some of the passengers were on deck throwing the ice about and they didn't take it at all seriously. When they realised that it was a real emergency it was all too late.'

Passenger Edith Haisman who was 16 years old at the time recalled: 'You could see the ice for miles

Below: **Drawing of the sinking of the *Titanic* by William Muller**

across the sea…nobody worried about it. Some of the people came up playing with the ice on deck and they wouldn't believe it, they said "No, she's unsinkable!" and they went back to bed…I thought it was wonderful to see the ice like that, you know…just wondered what happened, like everybody else…' **[Southampton Oral History Unit]**

Millvina: 'Our lifeboat was lowered to the water and moved away from the ship. It must have looked extraordinary to see the great *Titanic* sinking deeper and deeper into the water. Everyone was so surprised because it was supposed to be unsinkable. After the ship had gone, a woman in the boat became hysterical and screamed out, 'Where is my feather bed? I must get my feather bed,' My mother supposed that the lady had lost her husband and couldn't cope with the shock, as she seemed more concerned about her feather mattress than her husband!' (This is understandable when we consider that some of the poorest immigrants would have had very few possessions, and those they did take with them were often practical items like bedding and sewing machines, to help them start their new lives in America.)

'Later on, as the lifeboat was bobbing around in the night, they picked up a Chinese man from the freezing water who was floating on a raft. At first, the other women in the boat didn't want to let him in because they couldn't understand why he should be saved and not their husbands. But eventually they thought better of it.' Interestingly, fellow passenger Charlotte Collyer recalled this vivid incident too: 'We saw a floating door that must have torn loose when the ship went down. Lying upon it face down was a small Japanese [*sic*]. He had lashed himself with a rope to his frail craft using the broken hinges to make his knots secure. As far as we could see he was dead. The sea washed over him every time the door bobbed up and down, and he was frozen stiff. He did not answer when he was hailed and the officer hesitated about trying to save him. He had actually turned the boat round, but he changed his mind and went back. The Japanese was hauled on board and one of the women rubbed his chest while others his hands and feet. In less time than it takes to tell, he opened his eyes. He spoke to us in his own tongue, then seeing that we did not understand, he struggled to his feet,

*Contemporary representation of *Titanic*'s lifeboats being lowered.*

stretched his arms above his head, stamped his feet and in five minutes or so had almost recovered his strength.

One of the sailors near to him was so tired he could hardly pull his oar. The Japanese bustled over, pushed him from his seat, took the oar and worked like a hero until we were picked up. I saw Mr Lowe (5th Officer Lowe) watching him in open-mouthed surprise.'

My mother said later: 'Heroism and chivalry are the myths about the *Titanic*. That might have been true on the boat deck. But really, it was arrogance and madness that night…. madness.'

Above: **The rescue ship** *Carpathia.*   *Below:* **St Luke's Hospital New York.**

Rescue

'We were rescued by another ship called the *Carpathia* the following morning. My poor mother was worried sick about Vere and my father. Imagine her joy when she was reunited on the *Carpathia* with her little boy! It seems that another passenger had found him on the deck of the *Titanic*, scooped him up and put him into a lifeboat - which one nobody ever knew. My mother never found out who that kind person was - but he or she certainly saved my brother's life. Sadly, my father didn't make it. We never knew what happened to him but he perished along with all those other poor people that night.

Western Daily Mercury Tuesday, 23rd April, 1912 'Mr and Mrs Dean, of Branscombe near Sidmouth, with their two children were passengers in the *Titanic*. Mrs Dean and children were among the saved, but Mr Dean perished.'

My mother had a lot to think about on the way to New York. Her whole life's course had changed overnight. She couldn't possibly go to Kansas on her own with two small children. Who would look after her? How would she live? She decided that the best thing to do was to come back to England. However, when we arrived in New York the Red Cross sent us all to St Luke's Hospital in order to recuperate. My mother's health had suffered both physically and mentally. It had been such a terrible ordeal that we were there for six weeks.'

On the journey home aboard the White Star Liner *Adriatic* Millvina experienced her first taste of celebrity. A number of photographs were taken of her and the story appeared in the *Daily Mirror* on 12th May, 1912:

St. Lukes Hospital, New York City

S ASLEEP IN DECK CHAIRS ON WAY TO NEW YOF

Above: **Millvina and her Mother (on far right) in deck chair on the** *Carpathia.*   *Below:* **Millvina and Vere.**

[She] was the pet of the liner during the voyage, and so keen was the rivalry between women to nurse this lovable mite of humanity that one of the officers decreed that First and Second class passengers might hold her in turn for no more than ten minutes.

Journalists were later to establish that Millvina was actually the youngest passenger to survive the *Titanic* disaster which, of course, made her a very newsworthy and appealing subject.

Millvina: 'Instead of going back to London my mother decided to return to her parents in the New Forest. So, for my early years, I grew up in that lovely place, Bartley Farm. The American Red Cross gave the family $200 and they received $815 from other American Charities. In addition, the English *Titanic Relief Fund* gave my mother £40 and a pension of 23 shillings per week to take care of Vere and I. This helped to pay for our schooling: I went to the Gregg School for girls in Cumberland Place, Southampton while Vere went to the King Edward VI grammar school so, in an odd way, I owe a lot of my good education to the *Titanic*.'

Millvina with Bumblebee (in the pram) which was given to her in New York, and Vere with a cabbage in his wheelbarrow!

Life on Board the Titanic

Neither Millvina or her brother Bertram could remember the *Titanic* and since Ettie mostly refused to discuss either the ship or the disaster we can only make educated guesses at what life was like for the Dean family on board the ship based on evidence and accounts from other passengers in similar circumstances.

How did the Dean family get to the Titanic from London?

If the Dean family travelled on a normal scheduled service train they would have alighted at Southampton Terminus Station and taken a horse taxi into the docks with their luggage.

However, if they arrived on a special Boat Train from London Waterloo they would have gone straight through the Terminus Station across the road and into the docks. The train would have stopped at 43/44 berth and they would have alighted into the Dockside Sheds and Porters would have been engaged to take their luggage across to the ship perhaps 150 - 200 yards away.

On arriving at Southampton the Deans boarded the *Titanic* via a gangway to either D Deck forward or C Deck aft. Their ticket number was 2315 which cost

View of White Star dock in 1913. *Titanic*'s sistership, *Olympic*, is at Berth 43 on the far left.

£20 11s 6d. They were quickly checked over by a medical officer and then ushered into the maze of Third Class companionways to their cabin. Those first few hours must have been noisy, confusing and cramped. But at least the family were berthed together. The White Star Line routinely separated single men and women in Third Class by the entire length of the ship; women in the stern, men in the bow. The third class accommodation consisted of 2, 4, 6, 8 and 10 berth cabins. Later, after they had settled in, they would have had to find their own way to the saloons and general rooms and promenade spaces. After a brief stop at Cherbourg, France, the *Titanic* made its way to Queenstown (now Cobh) in Ireland.

As the *Titanic* left Queenstown an Irish passenger called Eugene Daly began to play 'Erin's Lament' on his uilleann bagpipes. Ettie and Bertram may well have caught a few bars of the melancholy tune and perhaps wondered if they had really made the right decision. If they did, it was too late because the next stop was New York. There could be no regrets, no turning back. They had to look to the future.

Ettie must have had her work cut out for her, looking after two very young children. This was an era before pre-packaged baby food, disposable nappies, handy wipes, and fold away push chairs. Looking after a small child and an infant in such strange surroundings would have been a full time job and an exhausting one. Without a crib the old tried and true method was often used to keep babies in bunks - the bottom bunk in Third Class was very low, ideal for small children - and with a chair pushed to the side as a makeshift rail, and propped pillows, an improvised crib could be created. Bathing either the children or herself would have been an effort for Ettie because in Third Class there were only two bathtubs, both of which were located in the stern - a long way to go to if you were quartered in the bow!

Washing baby nappies would have been a very trying task and drying them another problem altogether. There were no 'baby changing' facilities in steerage and not even a nursery or crèche for older

Titanic's last port of call, Queenstown in Southern Ireland, the final posting of letters from passengers and crew were sent from here. In the photograph below are the offices of the White Star Line.

children like Vere. Furthermore, there wasn't any kind of organised children's activities and certainly no specialised child care services.

The *Titanic* may have been the 'ship of dreams' for some but in Third Class it was anything but 'child friendly'!

What was the food like?

In some respects those first few days on board would have been quite unusual for Ettie and Bertram, because for one thing they were both completely free to do as they pleased. This would have been a 'holiday' period of relaxation (aside from the job of caring for the children) where their only obligation was to attend the three meals provided for them in one of the pleasant dining rooms. There were two of these, separated by a bulkhead and both were bright, enamel painted rooms livened up by colourful White Star Line framed posters on the wall. The Deans would have sat together at one of the long tables which were covered with linen tablecloths and would have had the chance to get to know their dining companions. Here they experienced the novelty of being waited on by a steward.

The food was plain, hearty and nourishing and a typical dinner menu might include: Vegetable Soup, Roast Pork with Sage and Pearl Onions, Green Peas, Boiled Potatoes, Plum Pudding with Sweet Sauce, Cabin Biscuits and Oranges.

While there were no specific menu options for children or babies in Third Class, on many liner menus of the period there could often be found farina, oatmeal, apple sauce, semolina, and other cereal based foods which would be ideal for infant food aboard. The food mill in the galley was a device often used to puree vegetables and fruits for invalids and no doubt was utilized for infants as well, though whether this service was extended to steerage passengers is debatable. A 1910 advertisement for glass nursing bottles with india rubber nipples shows that bottle feeding was an option for many mothers. Those women who chose not to breast feed their babies were well supplied with milk: the *Titanic* was carrying at least 1,500 gallons of it.

What did the Dean family do during the voyage?

Although the Third Class amenities were few, Ettie and Bertram had a number of limited options open to them to occupy their time between meals. For example, they were free to take the air on the forward or aft Third Class promenade spaces. The weather for those first four days at sea had been pleasantly sunny

---

White Star Line
RMS **Titanic** April 14, 1912

THIRD CLASS.

BREAKFAST.
OATMEAL PORRIDGE & MILK
SMOKED HERRINGS, JACKET POTATOES
HAM & EGGS
FRESH BREAD & BUTTER
MARMALADE   SWEDISH BREAD
TEA   COFFEE

DINNER.
RICE   SOUP
FRESH BREAD   CABIN BISCUITS
ROAST BEEF,   BROWN GRAVEY
SWEET CORN   BOILED POTATOES
PLUM PUDDING   SWEET SAUCE
FRUIT

TEA.
COLD MEAT
CHEESE   PICKLES
FRESH BREAD & BUTTER
STEWED FIGS & RICE
TEA

SUPPER.
GRUEL   CABIN BISCUITS
CHEESE

Third Class *Titanic* Menu.

---

and calm - ideal for strolling on deck. The poop deck at the stern of the ship offered some of the most spectacular views of the sea and was exclusively for Third Class use. Large numbers of steerage passengers gathered there during the day and no doubt the Deans spent some time there too.

The Deans, like all other Third Class passengers, were prevented from entering areas of the ship reserved for Second and First Class by latched or locked gates. These were used to curb the possibility of infectious diseases spreading - but also served to keep everyone in their place.

If the weather got too windy or cold for the children, Ettie and Bertram could take them inside and sit and relax in the warm General Room on C Deck. It is likely that Bertram explored the smoking room next door and may well have checked out the other licensed bar forward on D Deck. Being a barman himself he had more than just a passing interest and also probably took the opportunity to sample the ale!

Perhaps the couple found time to chat to other emigrating families and shared their plans, hopes and fears. There were plenty of people to talk to after all. On the *Titanic*'s maiden voyage there were approximately 713 Third Class passengers making their way to the 'New World'. Among the nationalities were English, Irish, Swedish, Finnish, German, Italian, Greek and Lebanese. And many of them, like the Deans, were emigrating to start afresh.

Ettie was a church goer and the whole family may well have attended a service for Third Class on Sunday, 14th, in the General Room. There is some debate about exactly where the church services were held for steerage passengers, but it seems likely that since the three classes on board the *Titanic* were segregated at all times they would not have been held in the opulent First Class Dining Room. There would be no reason for The White Star Line to change their rules just for divine worship. Ironically, that same night, many people from all classes would be praying together for their lives on the stern of the ship as the *Titanic* plunged to its watery grave.

What was the Entertainment like?

Ettie told Millvina that she had enjoyed listening to a band during the voyage. The White Star Line did not organise any kind of entertainment in Third Class so, the passengers made their own. This was most often a sing-song around the piano of popular music hall style songs which had a chorus that everyone could join in with. Eugene Daly certainly put his bagpipes to good use although, as school teacher Laurence Beesley noted, it wasn't to everyone's taste:

'Looking down astern from the boat deck … I often noticed how the Third Class passengers were enjoying every minute of the time; a most uproarious skipping game of the mixed double type was the great favourite, while 'in and out and roundabout' went a Scotchman (sic) with his bagpipes playing something that Gilbert said, "faintly resembled an air…"'

There seemed to be a lot of musicians among the steerage passengers and almost every night there were dances in the common areas of Third Class which must have created a jolly atmosphere.

On the night of the 14th there was a lively party in Third Class and it's possible that the Deans were there to witness at least some of the merriment. Sadly, it was to be the last night of carefree happiness for most of the assembled crowd.

How did the Dean family escape from the sinking Titanic?

The White Star Line had no formal evacuation policy in the event of an emergency and so when the *Titanic* began to take on water after colliding with an iceberg on the evening of Sunday 14th, at approximately 11.40pm, there was initially more confusion than panic. Nobody seemed to know what was going on and how bad it was. However, when water came seeping into the bow quarters of Third Class the question was academic. The survival instinct took over and people grabbed what belongings they could carry and started moving further aft to get away from the danger.

It was a long way up to the boat deck from the steerage quarters and while some passengers in Third Class were barred by locked gates, a few found their own way to the lifeboats with little or no help at all. But as Millvina was to observe years after the disaster,

Lowering a lifeboat.

Eva Hart with her parents.

'My father was quick on the uptake and got us out as soon as he knew something was wrong.' Ironically, Bertram's decisive action saved his wife and children but sadly, he was not able to save himself. The rule of the sea in 1912 was 'Women and Children First' and Bertram evidently did not attempt to go with the rest of his family.

Those deckside farewells must have been heart wrenching. But it was at this point that Vere got lost among the legs of the shuffling, anxious passengers. This would be every parent's worst nightmare. Bertram must have rushed his goodbyes and plunged back into the heaving crowds to search for him. Fortunately the boy had, of course, already been saved by another passenger. There is some evidence to suggest that Vere was actually placed in the same boat as Ettie and Millvina, but in the darkness and confusion they were unable to find each other. We can imagine Ettie crying out for her husband and her boy as the lifeboat creaked and juddered down to the water.

We shall never know what happened to Bertram Dean in those final, agonising moments. Some passengers crawled up to the stern of the ship and clung on, paralysed with fear, until the *Titanic* took the final plunge, others jumped. A considerable number of people simply prayed. From her lifeboat Ettie would have clearly heard the screams of the people in the water and then the horrible silence which followed it. It was this preternatural silence which was later

recalled with vivid accuracy by another survivor, Eva Hart: '…and finally the ghastly noise of the people thrashing about and screaming and drowning, that finally ceased. I remember saying to my mother once, 'How dreadful that noise was!' and I'll always remember her reply and she said , 'Yes, but think back about the silence that followed it… because all of a sudden the ship wasn't there, the lights weren't there and the cries weren't there.'
[Southampton Oral History Unit]

It was a long and harrowing night. Most people in the water died from hypothermia and exposure in the freezing cold water, but incredibly a handful did survive. Ettie recalled that the women in the lifeboat were reluctant to take on board a 'Chinaman' who was floating on a raft. Was this perhaps one of the Chinese sailors who was travelling on board as a passenger? His identity remains unclear, but his survival was a miracle, given that the greater part of those passengers exposed to those unforgiving conditions quickly succumbed.

What happened in the Aftermath?

That Vere was saved is in itself something of a miracle. His appearance on the *Carpathia* must have seeme more like a biblical resurrection when so many mothers were in mourning for a child. Fellow Third Class passenger Leah Aks could empathise with Ettie. She was also lucky enough to be reunited with her 10 month old baby Frank who had been lost, like Vere, in the confusion of the evacuation:

Washington Post: Thursday, 25th April, 1912

'[Frank was] recovered by the mother on the *Carpathia* after she had given [him] up for lost. The infant, having been taken by a frantic man, fell into the lap of a woman survivor in a lifeboat as it was tossed over the side of the *Titanic*. The mother, who fainted, was placed in another lifeboat.'

Had something like this happened to Vere in those last, desperate minutes?

But happy reunions like this were rare. What neither Ettie or anyone knew at that time, was just how far short the White Star Line had been in providing comprehensive care for every passenger on board. For, remarkably, there didn't seem to be any safety policy at all. There had been no lifeboat drill for the passengers, no safety talk and fatally, not enough lifeboats for everyone on board.

Ultimately, the bald statistics speak volumes. In the final tally it was discovered that only 25% of Third Class passengers had survived the *Titanic*'s maiden voyage. Shockingly, 52 out of the 79 children in Third Class were killed while more First Class men were saved than Third Class children.

On board the *Carpathia*, Ettie had no way of knowing this. All she knew was that she had lost her husband, the father of her children, and that the immediate future lay in ruins. Every possession she had was at the bottom of the Atlantic. There was only one possible thing to do now. Go home.

The *Mackay-Bennett* which had the grim task of picking up bodies from the North Atlantic.

Above: **The liner *Adriatic*.   *Below:* Millvina and her mother returning home on the *Adriatic*.**

After the *Titanic*:
The Quiet Years

'I was a highly strung child,' Millvina recalls. 'I've always thought it was because of my mother breast feeding me on the *Titanic* and being a mass of nerves. I suppose it did affect me in those early years without my knowing why. I was generally a good girl at school and didn't really get into much trouble and I was quite bright. I would burst into floods of tears if I got into trouble because it didn't happen that often!

By this time the *Titanic* was an awful memory for most people and nobody really talked about it. My mother never mentioned it at home and at school, even though the teachers would have known I had been on it, they didn't treat me differently in any way. People were much tougher about those types of things and just got on with life. I certainly never brought it up in conversation with my friends. However, on the odd occasion I was brought up short by my connection with it. To my disgust, people would sometimes point at me in the street as I went by and say, 'there goes Girlie Dean – she was on the *Titanic*!'

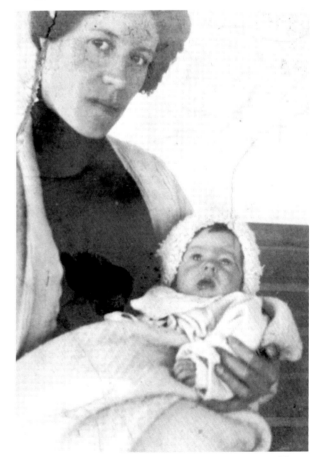

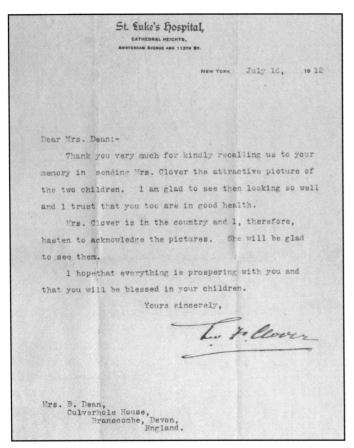

St. Luke's Hospital,
CATHEDRAL HEIGHTS,
AMSTERDAM AVENUE AND 113TH ST.

NEW YORK. July 16, 1912

Dear Mrs. Dean:-

Thank you very much for kindly recalling us to your memory in sending Mrs. Clover the attractive picture of the two children. I am glad to see them looking so well and I trust that you too are in good health.

Mrs. Clover is in the country and I, therefore, hasten to acknowledge the pictures. She will be glad to see them.

I hope that everything is prospering with you and that you will be blessed in your children.

Yours sincerely,

W. F. Clover

Mrs. B. Dean,
Culverhole House,
Branscombe, Devon,
England.

Above: Letter from St Luke's Hospital, New York, to Ettie who was staying with her in-laws in Branscombe. *Below:* Millvina. in a goat cart with her mother at Bartley Farm just after returning from America on the *Adriatic*.

'As for my mother, it was a subject which was closed for ever. Life had to go on and in those days people tended to put things behind them and look forward. She never forgot though. I remember many years after the disaster my mother and I opened an old trunk that had been locked for years, and inside was the blanket and other clothes that Vere and I wore when we arrived back in England after the disaster, but the moths had got to them and they just crumbled away.

When I was eight, in 1920, a vet called Leonard Burden came to see one of my grandfather's cows. He saw my mother as well and married her! She was still, after all, a very attractive lady. He was a kind man and they were very happy together. To be honest, I never really thought much about my real father. My grandfather was more like a father to me and for a while we lived with him at Bartley Farm.

Those were happy times. The Christmas's were always very special of course. I remember as a small child always having goose for Christmas dinner. I suppose it was because my grandfather, with whom we were living, kept geese on his farm. I'll also never forget riding in the horse and trap under star studded skies on crisp, frosty nights with just the clip clop of the horse's hooves the only sound. Later, the four of us moved to Southampton into my Stepfather's house in Millbrook Road. It had a two story veranda which overlooked the street and I loved it when the circus came to town. I would get up very early in the morning, and climb out onto the balcony to watch the animals and clowns parade right past our house, such bright colours - it was a wonderful sight!

I also remember playing 'Cowboys and Indians' with Vere and his friends. I always had to be the captured Indian maiden of course, and I'd be habitually tied to a post. However, one of the boys liked me, and so he would untie me in secret - but I had to pretend I untied myself!

We sometimes spent holidays with my father's parents in Branscombe, which was marvellous. I remember as a young girl looking out of the cottage window of my grandfather's house and seeing Archie, the farmers son, walking in the field with the plough. I sometimes walked up and down with him… Oh, it was heaven! Some time later he went to work at The Fountain Head Inn (still there today).

One year I took my friend Ethel there on holiday, to stay with an Aunt Rose who lived in a lovely house called Millers Lea. Aunt Rose had a tennis court and servants. Now, Ethel was Aunty Rose's favourite, because on Sunday mornings she would accompany

Right: Vere, Ettie and Millvina and dogs Willow and Fluffy in the garden of Bartley farm.

Above: **An idyllic setting in the New Forest.** *Below left:* **Number 55, Millbrook Road Southampton.**

her to church, while I went off to The Fountain Head Inn!

I have spent many holidays there since as it's such a lovely little village, very small. Only about 500 people there now and even less when my father lived there, but The Fountain Head Inn is still there! Ah, such lovely old memories!

My Stepfather was always good to us although I think Vere was a bit wary of him. I remember he would make me ask for things on his behalf where my Stepfather was concerned. But looking back, it's clear

that my Stepfather coped very well under the circumstances. My mother never liked going on the water after the *Titanic* disaster. The furthest she would go was to the Isle of Wight. I think one of the reasons she didn't discuss it was because after she remarried it wouldn't have done to dwell on the subject of her first husband. So, she pushed it very much into the background.

I didn't really have any ambitions as I grew up. My Stepfather had a large house with stables and there was always plenty to do with taking care of the animals there - which I loved. I left School at 16, and then I stayed home because there was ever so much to do. At Christmas time it was nothing to have 50 dogs and 50 cats in, with a dog in the scullery, one in the kitchen, one in the bathroom - they were everywhere! There was even a parrot and goldfish. I loved going to the cinema or theatre to see the latest Ivor Novello musical such as The Dancing Years or Glamorous Night, but it was a quiet life really, and quite uneventful.

After the Second World War broke out I was drafted into the Ordnance Survey

Above: **From left, Leonard Burden, Millvina's stepfather, her mother Georgette, grandfather George Light, grandmother Alice Light, nee Norbury, and Vere and Millvina. Taken in the garden of Bartley Farm. c.1923.**
Below: **A portrait of Millvina during the second world war.**

Office, we were initially given instruction in map drawing in the Southampton office, then sent to Hinchley Wood in Surrey and then to another building opposite Chessington Zoo. My abiding memory of that was the immense size of the building and how cold it was - awful! I have to admit that I wasn't very good at drawing but my boss liked me so he helped me out now and then. One of the draughtsmen used to say about us girls, 'Never were so many, paid so much, for doing so little!'

I was there for four years. I always remember at night in the blackout, all you could hear were the animals howling. Some of us girls boarded with a Mrs Tinsley, who was an awful cook. The only thing she could do was toast! Every morning we would run for the bus with a piece of toast in our hands. But it was such fun really. I made the best friends I ever had during the war. My days during the war were improved by a wonderful friend, Yolande Christopher, who was in the Ordnance Survey office with me.

The war years were interesting because although nobody had anything much to eat and there were so many restrictions, everyone seemed much more helpful and kind. We were all united by fear I suppose, but you could walk home in the blackout and feel quite safe. Oddly enough, those years were some of the happiest times of my life!

Still, everyone was so relieved when the war was over. I returned to Southampton, and my first job was in a tobacconist shop. I used to pass by it regularly, so one day I went in and said, 'Do you want anyone in your shop?' and the manager replied, 'As it happens I do.' So I said, 'Well, you've got me!' And I stayed there for three years until the son came out of the Army. I then got a job in the purchasing department of an engineering company called Vero Precision. There, I met someone who is still one of my dearest friends, Bruno Nordmanis who's been a constant friend ever since.

All through those years the *Titanic* disaster didn't effect me at all. But that was all to change after I retired!'

Above: Ettie being presented with a bouquet on her 90th birthday.
Below: Taking tea in the garden with Alastair Forsyth and Sheila Jemima.

Chapter Five
From Obscurity to Celebrity!

Interviewed in 1999 Millvina said: 'I came back to the New Forest to care for my mother and I've been here ever since. My mother had a quiet, happy life and died aged 96 on 16 September, 1975. She was an awfully nice person, more than a mother, she was a friend. Whatever other *Titanic* stories she had, she took to her grave because to the best of my knowledge she never really gave interviews about it and didn't want to be reminded of it.'

Millvina's post retirement life was initially one of almost complete anonymity. She was happy living quietly in the modest bungalow she had shared with her mother. There, she took particular delight in tending her garden, and taking walks in the New Forest. Her love of gardening came from her childhood. : 'My Mother was concerned about my nose always being stuck in a book, so she took me to the Doctor who advised her to give me a little patch of garden to grow things in.'

Then, in 1985, an event occurred which was to change her solitude and privacy forever: the wreck of the *Titanic* was discovered.

Interest in the *Titanic* exploded once again all over the world and, naturally, the media turned to the handful of remaining survivors for soundbites and reminiscences. Some survivors regarded this revival of '*Titanic* Mania' as extreme bad taste while others embraced the opportunities it afforded them to meet new people, talk about the disaster, give lectures, open exhibitions and travel abroad.

The last time the press had taken so much interest in Millvina was on the deck of the *Adriatic* in 1912 when she had slept on and off through the event! Now, at the age of 73 she was ready to enjoy new challenges and experiences. Once again the *Titanic* was going to change her life and things were never going to be the same again.

In 1987 Millvina attended a memorial service in Southampton to mark the 75th anniversary of the disaster.

Dozens of interviews and invitations followed and now Millvina found herself in great demand. In 1992 she attended the opening of the *Titanic* Voices exhibition at Southampton Maritime Museum with her friends Eva Hart and Edith Haisman - who were also child passengers on the *Titanic*.

In 1995 Millvina made her first trip to America where she addressed 600 New York and New Jersey schoolchildren about the disaster.

Millvina and her good friend Bruno Nordmanis.

However, it was not all smooth sailing: 'When we arrived in Boston it appeared that I did not have the correct entry papers, so they weren't going to let me in! It was terribly embarrassing. We were getting really worried, until a female migration official asked what the matter was. I explained to her why I was visiting – and of course that I was a *Titanic* survivor. Well, after that, her whole manner changed. She said. 'Honey, you've suffered enough! Go and enjoy yourself!' I was so relieved I threw my arms around her and kissed her!'

After the discovery of the wreck of the *Titanic* it was perhaps inevitable that salvage attempts would

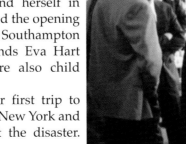

Millvina attending one of the many *Titanic* conventions.

take place to retrieve objects from it.

However, it was a hotly divisive issue, not least because of the questionable moral ethics concerning removing personal items from the wreck site. The survivors themselves were divided about it too. Some of them applauded the engineering and skill involved in photographing and recovering items while others were utterly disgusted with what they regarded as grave robbing. Millvina had mixed feelings about it. In a letter to the British Titanic Society she wrote:

'1994 has been a momentous year for me. In March I was at the National Maritime Museum with [fellow *Titanic* survivor] Edith Haisman, for a conference regarding the artefacts. We were besieged by the mass of media people - there seemed to be hundreds of them. The Admiral of the Fleet chaired the meeting.

TV crews from all over the world descended on the Maritime Museum, Japanese, Chinese, Brazilian etc. etc. Apart from a short break for lunch I was standing from 9am - 5.30pm. I have to admit though, I loved it all.'

Left: **Eva Hart, Edith Haisman and Millvina at Southampton Maritime Museum in 1992.**

Below: **Alastair Forsyth, Millvina, Sheila Jemima and Donald Hyslop at the 'Titanic Voices' book signing at the National Maritime Museum.**

She was back to open the National Maritime Museum's *Titanic* artefact exhibition the following year and gave her opinion about it in another letter to the British Titanic Society.

'I had not been to London since the war but have now been there three times since last October!

Before the exhibition opened I was asked by dozens of people what my thoughts were on bringing up the artefacts from the wreck.

I said as long as they were taken from the sea bed and not off the wreck, I thought that was acceptable. They are of such great interest to people all over the world and I feel are of historical value.'

However, as the years went on and deep sea technology advanced, the wreck itself has inevitably been plundered for artefacts too. In July 2000 Millvina told a reporter from the Southern Daily Echo:

'I think it is all wrong. I think the ship should be left in peace. Any bits and pieces that have come out from the ship on the seabed - that is alright. But to go into the ship - no, that's all wrong.'

Scientists argue that the ship is deteriorating so rapidly that the recovery of items from within the wreck is a race against time. Pro-salvage enthusiasts maintain that they are preserving history for future generations. Other people declare it is bad taste. Either way, it is certain that this will remain an emotive issue for the remaining survivors and their families for many years to come.

Millvina signing autographs at a *Titanic* Convention in Southampton.

In July 2001 an American couple, David Leibowitz and Kimberley Miller were married on board a tiny submersible resting on the deck of the *Titanic*. 'Nothing but a publicity stunt - and a rather tacky one at that!' said Millvina with scorn when she heard the news. But Mr Leibowitz had no regrets: 'We don't really regard this as a gravesite,' he said. The ceremony was presided over by Captain Ronald Warwick, master of the Cunard liner *QE2*, by radio link from the Russian research vessel, *Akademik Keldysh* four kilometres above the wreck.

Millvina has even been offered a free ticket to go down to the wreck site in a submersible. 'Not on your life!' she says firmly. 'Not even for a million pounds!'

There have been a number of proposals to build full scale replicas of the *Titanic* for commercial cruises. These stories are always newsworthy and inevitably, Millvina is asked to comment. 'One *Titanic* is enough.'

she says grimly. 'It would be an awful shame. The *Titanic* should now be left to the history books and people should not cash in on something that cost lives. The *Titanic* was not a happy ship, but these companies trying to make a fortune out of such a tragedy is wrong.

In my opinion it is tempting fate and being insensitive by trying to recreate the ship. Besides, I think superstition alone will stop people booking on any replica ship except those with a morbid fascination with it. We don't need another, thank you!' And that is her final word on the subject.

One unforeseen aspect of her new found celebrity following the discovery of the wreck was the increasing volume of post which would now drop onto her door mat every morning. Since 1987 she has found that she is in great demand to sign autographs for books, postcards, prints, photographs and other ephemera. Often, people who, for whatever reason, feel a strong connection with the *Titanic* write to her because they want some kind of contact with a real *Titanic* survivor. After giving it some thought she believes she understands the reason:

'I've been told that I'm living history, that for many people I somehow represent the *Titanic*. I expect that's why they want to write to me. Sometimes people get very emotional and burst into tears when I meet them. All I can say is, 'there, there' and hope they'll be alright.'

But the reality of encountering a person who was actually on the *Titanic* can be an overwhelming experience for some. Millvina has met people who start sobbing when they meet her or who are rendered speechless because they are so excited. When she did a book signing at Greenwhich Maritime Museum in 1995, a little four year old came up to her and asked her if she was 'still alive?'! A few people feel a compulsion to touch her, hold her hand, or put their arm around her after the briefest of introductions. In March, 1990, Schoolboy Paul Fairley realised a long held ambition by meeting not one but four survivors, including Millvina, at the unveiling of one of the musician memorials in Southampton. He described it later in an article for the British Titanic Society as quite simply, 'The best day I have ever had.'

The type of mail Millvina receives can range from formal invitations to the intensely personal; correspondents of all ages, race and creed from all around the globe. There is always plenty to get through. On returning from one trip abroad in the mid 1990s she observed:

'...I thought it would be a peaceful time, but not so. This morning letters arrived from Germany, Ulster and America. My pen is getting worn out!'

Some letters provide some welcome light relief from the hundreds of demands for autographs and lengthy reminiscences. In 1996 she wrote:

'I have just had a letter from a Chinese school-master, who wants to write a book about the *Titanic* for his countrymen. He wrote a very good letter but I didn't much like the apology for writing to me because "...you very venerable and infirm". I was going to try using his Chinese address but apparently if I'd made the slightest mistake it would mean something entirely different so I changed my mind!'

At other times it was a relief just to receive something that had nothing to do with the *Titanic*. In 2004 she wrote:

'Today, I was amazed to receive a letter, not about the *Titanic* but about the last war! Apparently the writer, a schoolgirl, is doing a project about it. Quite a change...!'

While other replies throw up some welcome surprises:

'I had a letter recently from a young man in Germany who was organising a German/Irish *Titanic* evening. He asked me if I would write a small note for his menu, so of course, I did. He was so pleased he sent me some home-made cookies from his restaurant!'

Some requests border on the downright bizarre:

'A young man wrote and asked me if he could be my adopted grandson which was a rather an odd request. Stranger still, I agreed!'

In 2006 Millvina was bemused to open a letter which began: 'I'm Captain Smith of the *Titanic*. May I come and see you Miss Dean?'
He was duly invited to afternoon tea:

'So he came, a very big, tall man, about 6'4", and looking exactly like Captain Smith, except for the height, of course. He apparently goes to exhibitions and such like as "Captain Smith", and really thinks he is! There are people like that. I met Sherlock Holmes once, deerstalker hat and all. He told me he still lived in Baker Street. I just humour them; as long as they're happy!'

Other people write with pleas for Millvina to write essay length answers to all sorts of questions pertaining to the *Titanic*. Many just want her signature to add to their collections or to sell. There is a brisk

Captain Smith with his dog on the *Olympic*.

business for Millvina material and daily, it seems, the pile of mail grows and grows.

Christmas is always a time when her post bag increases ten fold:

'As usual I had hundreds of Christmas cards,' she wrote in 2004. I was quite inundated. I even had a basket of goodies from Australia! Now I am trying to answer all those letters...'

Any idea of having a printed response to ease her correspondence is dismissed out of hand:

'I couldn't possibly do that. People want me to write to them personally. It would be bad manners to do otherwise. It just takes me rather longer these days as there are so many to deal with!'

In 2000, Millvina received a plea which she could not ignore and once more connected her directly with the past. The *Nomadic* is the last White Star Line ship afloat, built in 1911 by Harland & Wolff, for many years it tendered passengers onto the great liners, including *Titanic*, in Cherbourg. After the Second World War it became a floating restaurant called *Ingenieur Minard* on the River Seine in Paris but the ravages of time had taken their toll and by early 2000 it seemed as if the historic ship was headed for the junk pile.

Millivina had actually visited the *Nomadic* in 1995 and been interviewed aboard her by Channel One - France's largest network. Five years later a campaign was begun to save the ship and Millvina was only too delighted when she was asked to be involved, but worried about the timing and how effective she could be:

'This morning I've had a letter from France with papers for me to sign to keep the *Nomadic* from the scrap heap. I'm delighted to help, but wish it had arrived when the [British Titanic Society in 2000] Convention was on because everyone would have been able to sign it: but what can I do now? It's so difficult, where can I get people to sign?'

Thankfully, enough money was raised and the vessel is now undergoing full restoration in Belfast. Over the years Millvina has also noted a recurring theme in many of her male correspondent's letters which she finds rather amusing:

'It's amazing how many men write to me for my signature and say they've been very interested in the *Titanic* since they

Above: **Millvina accompanies Edith Haisman at the National Maritime Museum, Greenwich, London in 1995.**

Left: Ingenieur Minard **(formerly the** *Nomadic***) tendering the Cunard liner** *Queen Mary* **at Cherbourg in the 1950s.**

were six years old. It's so funny. It's always six years!'

Some requests came not by post but by other means:

'I have had hundreds of telephone calls since the film [James Cameron's *Titanic*] came out. One was from Columbia at 10pm. A voice said, 'This is Colombia radio. We go all over South America right to Miami and will you please give an interview Miss Millvina at 11.20pm?' I said, 'No I'm in bed at 11pm! But I was persuaded (I am a soft touch) and went to bed at 1am. Another call which surprised me was when, completely out of the blue, I was asked what I thought about the situation in Africa. 'Serious,' I replied coolly, 'Very serious!'

As recently as 2005 Millvina could say, 'I'm still doing interviews. A few weeks ago I had six Japanese people interviewing me for a *Titanic* documentary, and then a few days after, three Frenchmen came, doing the same thing.'

Millvina has been interviewed by school children, amateur historians, local journalists, reporters from the national and international press - both tabloid and broad sheet - including The New York Times, The Washington Post, Daily Mail and The Telegraph. She is nearly always featured in her local paper, the Southern Daily Echo whenever anything *Titanic* related comes up in the news. Her story is often repeated in magazines (particularly around the anniversary of the disaster) and every quarter she contributes an open letter to the British Titanic Society journal, The Atlantic Daily Bulletin. On the occasion of her 90th birthday she wrote: 'It will soon be my birthday, I can't believe I'll be 90! It seems most extraordinary. I thought it would be a quiet affair, but now the BBC are going to be at my small party in a hotel, and relatives are coming from Canada, friends from America and the Continent, and of course England. A quiet affair!'

She is also discussed and written about at length on various *Titanic* themed internet sites and chat rooms.

Above: **Millvina and Bruno centre of attention.**
Below: **Who's interviewing who? Millvina on stage.**

Millvina and her brother Vere at a *Titanic* event.

There is hardly a year that goes by when she is not called upon to comment on some new development connected with the *Titanic*.

Millvina has also been a celebrity guest for famous chat show hosts such as Larry King and Geraldo (USA) Vera (Vienna) and Terry Wogan (UK), none of whom seem to ruffle her calm and gracious demeanour in the slightest. The only type of interviews she dislikes are those done by satellite because she can't see the person she is talking to. However, she concedes that this is a minor quibble. 'High or low, I like most people,' she says frequently. 'I just hope they don't think I'm conceited!'

Chapter Six
Millvina's brother Vere

Vere with a *Titanic* model made by his son Frank.

Millvina's brother Vere (or 'Bert' as he was known outside the family) had, like his sister, very little to do with the *Titanic* for most of his life but as he grew into old age he developed a casual interest which increased after the discovery of the wreck. He too was surprised and flattered in later life to be asked to sign autographs, give interviews, attend *Titanic* conventions and special ceremonies and give the occasional talk both in the UK and in America.

'I don't remember anything of the actual event,' he said. 'But I have lived it over and over again as my mother told me, as I read books and magazines about the events.'

When Vere was working at Husbands Shipyard in Southampton he met a man called Charles Beauchamp who had been in the same lifeboat as him all those years before: 'You must have been the little

boy,' he said, to Vere's astonishment. They became good friends.

The *Titanic* disaster affected Southampton badly, over 649 crew members lost their lives in the disaster, and it touched the lives of many people in the Town, directly either through the loss of a relative or indirectly by other means. Vere's wife Dorothy Dean (nee Sinclair) was also from Southampton and also had a connection with the *Titanic*. Her father had purchased one of the music shops owned by *Titanic* victim Henry Price Hodges.

The Dean family were not the only New Forest family to be affected by the *Titanic* tragedy. In the nearby village of Fritham the Hickman Family lost three brothers, Leonard, Stanley and Lewis who were travelling to Canada as second class passengers. Accompanied by four friends, who were also from the

Above: **The Hickman family. Back row 3rd from left Leonard, second row 5th from left Lewis and next to him Stanley, all perished in the disaster.** *Courtesy: Mr B Hickman* *Below:* **Edith Haisman, Millvina, Vere and Eva Hart on the occasion of the unveiling of a memorial to the musicians on the *Titanic* in Southampton in 1990.**

New Forest, they were travelling on a single ticket at a cost of £73.10s. Tragically, all seven men lost their lives in the disaster.

On 7th March, 1990, Vere, along with Millvina and *Titanic* survivors Edith Haisman and Eva Hart were guests of honour at the site of the Old Southampton Library (which was then the new office building of the Municipal Mutual Insurance Company) for the unveiling of a memorial to the musicians who died in the disaster.

Vere died on the anniversary of the sinking on 15th April, 1992. The Southern Daily Echo carried the story:

Survivor Dies on *Titanic* Anniversary

Titanic survivor Bert Dean died last night - 80 years almost to the hour that the ship hit an iceberg on its maiden voyage.

Bert, who was 82, died in his sleep at Moorgreen Hospital Southampton.

'He was a gentle, caring man who was only too pleased to share his memories and give time to anyone interested in the *Titanic*.' said Brian Ticehurst, Southampton based editor of

the British Titanic Society's newsletter.

Bert, together with his baby sister and mother, were plucked from a lifeboat by the *Carpathia* and taken to hospital in New York. His father was among the 1,503 who perished.

Bert's sister, Millvina, who was a nine week old baby in 1912 is the youngest survivor from the *Titanic*…'

With his death, another link to the *Titanic* disaster had gone forever.

Chapter Seven
Belfast and Cobh

Throughout the 1990s Millvina was in great demand to attend *Titanic* related functions. Often the past and present would collide in unexpected ways. In 1996 she was invited to Belfast, where the *Titanic* had been constructed, to attend a rather special dinner given by the American based Titanic Historical Society:

'…We went to Harland and Wolff's [the company which oversaw the building of the *Titanic*] for dinner and had the same dinner menu that was served to the First Class passengers on the *Titanic* on the evening of April 14th, 1912. There was a musical accompaniment by the Ulster Royal Regiment Military band. Quite enchanting.'

Millvina would attend a number of these 'Last Dinners on the *Titanic*' and she would sometimes quip that at last her ticket had been upgraded! Her costumes, she noted were usually very grand: 'I had to go to a costumiers to be measured. I loved my long dress and feathered hat, and I have never seen more elegant people. Those clothes were not, of course, practical, but were so delightful.'

Sometimes the table talk could take an interesting turn as Millvina recalled: 'I was having dinner with the Director of the National Maritime Museum, and he asked for a jug of water and started to pour me a glass. I said, 'No thank you.' He looked a bit surprised and replied, 'But Millvina you must drink it, it's so

The quay at Cobh, called Queenstown at the time of the *Titanic*'s brief encounter with the harbour here.

The next day there was a reception with Deputy Lord Mayor followed by a Farewell Dinner in the Grand Ballroom of the Europa Hotel:

'Music was played by a violinist,' wrote Millvina, 'and a pianist. They played 'Autumn' at the end, a most beautiful haunting piece of music, and I was amazed to hear that that was the last piece of music played on the *Titanic* and not, as is always thought, 'Nearer My God To Thee'.'

healthy.' I told him "Healthy? My great Aunt died at 99, my grandmother was 95 and my Mother was 96, and they never drank water. As my grandmother used to say, 'Water is for washing, wine is for drinking!'

Cobh

In late 1996 Millvina travelled to Cobh in southern Ireland which, of course, has its own *Titanic* connection. This was the *Titanic*'s last port of call before heading off across the Atlantic and into the history books. Many of the passengers boarding there were poor Irish immigrants in Third Class. Family members who had said goodbye to loved ones boarding the ship just days earlier, streamed back into the seaside town, as if that would somehow make the impending news of the passengers' fate easier. When the news arrived with the names of the dead, grief swept through the town. A memorial service for the victims was held at St Coleman's Cathedral. Although not everyone who boarded at Cobh was Irish, the loss was felt all over the country, especially in Cobh.

Millvina recalled later: 'I was given the real VIP treatment there. I was met off the plane by the Mayor

The elegant Café Parisien on board *Titanic*.

of Cobh and then a Piper in full regalia piped us in to the Airport Arrival Lounge!' The cathedral bells rang a carillon, which was very emotional, then they played Come back to Erin.'

In 1998, Millvina was asked back to perform a task more associated with royalty:

'I cut the first turf for the foundation of a *Titanic* restaurant. I don't think it will be ready for some time though, there's so much work to be done. Cobh is one of my favourite places. It's so unspoiled.'

The restaurant, called 'Titanic', had been the brain child of lottery winning Irishman Vincent Kiearney and was located in the old White Star Line offices facing the harbour. (the restaurant has since closed).

Rooms were fitted out with vintage liner fittings including wood panelling and period lighting. The wash basins in the ladies toilets were taken from the *Titanic*'s sister ship, *Olympic* and floor tiles from the *Britannic*. There was even to be a replica of the *Titanic*'s First Class Café Parisien. Despite inevitable delays Millvina was back on Sunday, 20th August, 2001 to see it finished for herself:

'At last the restaurant was opened - very successfully. It is quite lovely, and I was very flattered to have a 'Dean' room there with a portrait of me.'

The best selling Irish writer, Pete McCarthy wrote about this event in his light hearted travelogue, The Road to McCarthy:

'The Dean Room has huge wooden-framed windows, salvaged from a local house when they were discarded in favour of that maintenance-free UPVC that turns grey and falls out after 15years. We were able to look out on the tugboats passing on the water outside, and beyond them the harbour mouth through which so many - convicts and famine victims, unmarried women and unemployed men … passed on their way to uncertain and mostly unrecorded futures. I had a seat next to Millvina, a trim and sparky woman who was a nine-week old baby when the ship went down. I felt awkward and didn't know what to talk about. Should I ask her if she enjoyed the movie? Would she be amused by the ice cubes in the urinals? She turned out to be good company, and well used to being trotted out for Titanic-related events.

'I think they think I am the *Titanic* in America [she said]. Some of them are obsessed. One man wrote asking for a lock of my hair.

'So what did you think of that?'

'I thought he was a nutcase."

… It was hard to hear because people kept coming through to peer at Millvina, which didn't seem to bother her… She's a nice lady…'

Millvina was also afforded a Civic Reception by Cobh Urban District Council at the Town Hall for her 'outstanding interest in RMS *Titanic* and to the benefits which had accrued to Cobh'. Acting town clerk, Paraig Lynch said:

'Millvina is a relatively frequent visitor here and has, in the past, expressed her warm feelings for the town. We do not have the option of giving her the freedom of the town, so this is the highest honour available to an individual.'

Chapter Eight
More Titanic Connections

While on a trip to New York in 1995 Millvina had the pleasure of presiding over a rather special ceremony:

'I presented plaques to the Red Cross, Salvation Army and the Metropolitan Insurance Company because they all helped in the aftermath of the *Titanic* disaster, and are, of course, still helping in all disasters.

I also went to see the wharf where the rescue ship the *Carpathia* berthed. Sadly, it is now derelict…'

That same year Millvina visited Paris for a few days. During her stay a reunion was organized with fellow *Titanic* survivors Louise La Roche and Micheal Navratil who had both, like Millvina, been small children at the time of the disaster:

'Louise was extraordinary,' recalls Millvina, 'quite the smallest person I have ever seen. She was absolutely tiny, but such a dear. Our visit coincided with Bastille Day and we watched a wonderful display of fireworks from our hotel near the Eiffel Tower. Oh, the changing colours of blues, reds, greens, golds! Everything was quite magnificent. We could see all over Paris. It was an unforgettable night.

I was interviewed with Louise on board a floating restaurant which had once been the tender *Nomadic*. Louise and her family had used it to board the *Titanic* in 1912.'

It was a whirlwind visit but none the less Millvina managed to fit in a special reception at the Paris Hilton as well as the more usual tourist attractions such as Notre Dame, the Arc de Triomph, and the Place de la Concorde. At the Louvre she saw three of the most famous works of art displayed there: the Mona Lisa, the Venus de Milo and the Winged Victory of Sumothrace.

Millvina has always enjoyed seeing new places. Following the release of the hugely successful motion picture, James Cameron's *Titanic*, she was in more demand than ever. In fact before the showing of the film at Harbour Lights Cinema in Southampton, she gave an interview on the stage before an invited audience, although did not stay to see the film.

Millvina with Captain Warwick and his wife Kim. Photo signed as 'Master of *QE2* 26th June 1999'.

Millvina in a favourite outfit - a green silk dress which she bought to wear on her visit to Ireland.

Indeed, in 1997 alone she travelled to California, Mexico, Hamburg, Switzerland and New York. Since 1985 she has also visited Scotland, Northern Ireland, Eire, Paris, Vienna, Norway, Estonia, Finland, Denmark, St Petersburg, Belgium, Austria, Canada and much of America. In Paris, Millvina watched a firework display from President Mitterand's Penthouse. Only illness prevented her from making the journey to Australia. 'People spoil me, so of course I love it!' she often comments. Wherever she goes she is often presented with small tokens of appreciation but one of the most unusual came from a trip to American were she was made an honorary member of the FBI.

In 1996 Millvina was asked to attend one ceremony which she uncharacteristically turned down - but for good reason.

'I decided against going to the *Titanic* wreck on the special memorial cruise. I thought it would have been too emotional for me.'

Later in Boston she met someone else with a very interesting *Titanic* link:

'We had a very nice evening in a lovely hotel called Le Meridian with some friends we met earlier. One was a relation of Captain Lord of the *Californian*.' It was a poignant meeting for, as every *Titanic* buff knows, the *Californian* is the ship that might or might not (historical accounts conflict) have stood by while the *Titanic* foundered.

Millvina has always had a love of travelling by ship and her favourite by far is the Cunard liner *QE2* which she has sailed on a number of times. In August, 1997 she took a week long cruise on the Carnival Cruise Line's *Jubilee* as a guest of the Titanic Historical Society after attending their annual convention. She has also enjoyed cruises on smaller ships such as the P&O *Victoria* (ex *Kungsholm*) which she likes because of their size. 'I find some of these modern cruise ships so enormous and a little bit overwhelming!' she says.

Curiously, when Millvina was a little girl Ettie would sometimes take her down to Southampton docks to see the ships. In those days it was also possible to purchase a ticket for a small fee and take a guided tour of many of the liners in port. Millvina recalled these excursions with fondness in February 2004:

'I remember my mother took me on board the *Titanic's* sister ship, the *Olympic* and the Cunard liner, the *Berengaria*. But the ones I loved best were the Union Castle ships which were really elegant.'

When asked if she found it strange or unsettling going through *Olympic's* public rooms and decks (which were practically identical to the *Titanic's*) she said, 'Not in the least. I never gave it a moment's thought! It's so odd because I just never even thought about the *Titanic* in those days.'

In October, 2000, Millvina had the chance to be the captain of a ship herself - albeit rather briefly:

'On a visit to Canada we crossed the St Lawrence River by ferry. I was allowed to try my hand at steering. Not very successfully I'm afraid!'

Berengaria, Leviathan and *Olympic* **moored at Southampton's Eastern Docks.**

An ankle and an adventure!

Illness is usually the only reason for Millvina refusing an invitation. Just before Christmas in 1997 she wrote to the British Titanic Society a 'tale of woe' describing a recent misfortune. Luckily, her dear friend Bruno was on hand to help, but it turned out to be quite an adventure!

'I fell down and badly hurt my ankle. So off I had to go to the Southampton General Hospital for an X-ray. What a time we had there.

Unfortunately neither Bruno nor I knew our way around and it took us a very long time to find the car park. Eventually we did, but it was dark and I stepped out into a large puddle and it was pouring with rain…

We found Casualty quite easily. I then had to wait to be assessed. After three hours we set off to find the X-ray department, Bruno pushing me in a wheel chair. It was a very perilous journey as we were going very fast from side to side, nearly knocking people over, until a nurse told Bruno that he should be pushing the chair the other way round! From then on all was well, and we at last found our objective. I was X-rayed and it was discovered that no bones were broken after all.

Time to go home and Bruno left me in the chair and went to get the car, and I waited, and waited and waited. Where on earth was he? After 20-25 minutes he arrived. It turned out that he hadn't been able to find his way back to where I was waiting. Was I pleased to get home!'

Southampton

Since the discovery of the wreck of the Titanic Millvina has been in great demand to preside over the opening of exhibitions and the unveiling of plaques in Southampton. These events are always covered by the Southern Daily Echo and over the years their archive of "Millvina Material" has become quite considerable.

In recognition of her civic duties, Millvina has had a road named after her ('Millvina Close'). 'It is quite extraordinary to have a Road named after you,' observed Millvina after the event, 'most people have their names used when they are dead!'

In 2005 Southampton City Council even named a bus after their famous 'daughter':

Southern Daily Echo
Naming Gives Bus a Titanic Link
A double decker bus has been named after *Titanic* survivor Millvina Dean.

Right: **Eastern Docks Memorial unveiling with the harbour master and Bishop of Southampton**

Millvina's name now adorns the top of the number U1 bus that operates between Southampton University's Oceanography Centre and the Highfield University Campus via the city centre. The route passes through Winn Road where the captain of the liner, Captain Edward Smith, lived.

When asked by reporters about it she replied: 'It's lovely! It was completely amazing to be asked to have a bus named after me. At first I could not understand what it was all about but I think it's a very good idea. … This will help people remember the *Titanic* and all those who died.'

In April 1993 Millvina received an invitation to unveil a plaque in memory of the *Titanic* victims in the gardens of Ocean House, Southampton Docks, which overlooks berth 43 - *Titanic*'s original departure point.

The *Titanic* had arrived at Southampton on 4th April 1912 to much local enthusiasm, not least because of all the job prospects she brought with her in what was a hard time of unemployment in the city. Five days later news of the disaster reached the city and the people of Southampton were plunged into mourning.

The British Titanic Society had played a key role in having the memorial installed and Millvina (who is an honorary member) was only too delighted to be asked to be involved:

Peter Boyd Smith reported the event to the British Titanic Society journal 'The Atlantic Daily Bulletin':

'…April 10th was a cold grey day, and at 12 noon a group of 70 plus people assembled at the head of the Ocean Dock to watch *Titanic* survivor Millvina Dean unveil a granite memorial in memory of the passengers and crew of the *Titanic*.

The introductory address was given by Captain Ridge, who is the port's senior harbourmaster, and

then Millvina lifted a White Star house flag and said how honoured she was to perform the ceremony. Canon Roberts who is the Missions to Seamens Chaplain then said a prayer of dedication followed by a prayer for seamen everywhere, which ended the ceremony.

Among the crowd were several people whose relatives were on the Titanic…'.

In April, 2000, Millvina was asked her opinion about the idea of having a dedicated *Titanic* Museum in the city. It was an idea she embraced warmly:

'I think it is nice because the *Titanic* has become part of history. After all, she sailed from Southampton. It would also help to keep the memory of the people alive of those who died.'

The City are proposing to build a new Heritage Centre which will tell the story of the *Titanic*, and put on display more of the wonderful *Titanic* collections currently held in the Museum archives.

One occasion Millvina very much enjoyed in Southampton was a special concert in April, 2002 which was reported by the Southern Daily Echo:

Above: **Millvina is accompanied by well-known** *Titanic* **historian Brian Ticehurst during a Southampton Convention.** *Below:* **Unveiling a plaque on the old White Star Line building in Canute Road, Southampton with Councillor Derek Burke.**
Courtesy Robin Jones. Digital South

An Ovation for *Titanic* Survivor

Titanic survivor Millvina Dean received a standing ovation when she appeared at a schools concert at Southampton's Guildhall.

The show was organised by the Southampton School's Music Association and featured a choir made up from pupils from secondary schools and sixth forms in the city.

The highlight of the night was a performance by the Southampton Youth Pops Orchestra of 'Symphonia Titanica' which is based on the 1912 tragedy.

Miss Dean was guest of honour at the show which attracted 600 people.

Following the moving performance, she received a standing ovation when she went on stage to thank the youngsters.

Compere John Smith said: 'It was a real tear jerker and show stopper when she was on stage and it shows the pull that the *Titanic* still has.'

Millvina has close connections with the Southampton Martime Museum and has opened a number of their *Titanic* exhibitions - most notably the splendid 'Titanic Voices' exhibition with Edith Haisman and Eva Hart in 1992.

In 2002 she was in Southampton again for another moving tribute:

Millvina: 'On 15th April I unveiled a plaque on the old White Star Offices in Canute Road. It was to commemorate the

Left: Anxiously waiting for news. The scene at the White Star Line's offices in Canute Road shortly after the disaster. Names of those who were lost and saved were posted up on the railings.

Titanic has become a myth in a way now and there's some mystique about it because it was supposed to be unsinkable.'

In August, 2002, she was back at the Maritime Museum to mark the 90th anniversary of the disaster with the opening of a new exhibition there.

'I'm always amazed by the amount of interest people show.' she told the press, 'But I'm sure it will continue as children are still fascinated by the tragedy, and interest will go on for a while longer… I'm flattered that people want to know more, but I was young at the time and it's a long time ago that it's hard to remember sometimes.'

fact that this was the place where all the relatives of the people on the *Titanic* waited for news of their loved ones. There was a crowd of people there to watch me do it.'

In April, 1912, these offices had been witness to scenes of joyous relief and intense despair and sorrow. As information trickled in, lists of names were posted outside on the office notice board of who was lost and who was saved. Sometimes the mis-spelling of names caused distress and confusion. Many people stayed there for several days waiting for news. The cost in human life was terrible for the local crew and their families. An incredible 549 crewmen and women with a Southampton address perished in the disaster.

The Daily Mirror reported at the time:

> 'The gloom which hangs over Southampton is intensified daily and the agonising scenes at the docks could move the hardest hearts to compassion.'

In the Chapel, Northam and St Marys parishes, many households lost their only breadwinner and had to rely on handouts from the *Titanic* Relief Fund which was set up after the disaster for the benefit of widows and orphans.

80 years later Millvina stood outside Canute Chambers and said:

'I wanted to come here and do this. After all, the

Indeed, it appears as though interest in the *Titanic* simply grows and grows. Millvina speculates on what the Centenary will bring:

'I can't imagine what they'll expect me to do for the 100th anniversary! We'll just have to wait and see.'

One idea put forward by the council is for a 100 foot high tower to commemorate the disaster and to pay tribute to local merchant seamen. If completed, visitors will be able to 'look out across the docks to the berth where *Titanic* left on her doomed maiden voyage in 1912.' Millvina thinks it's a wonderful idea:

'Southampton should do a lot more to remember the *Titanic*,' she commented in July 2001 in an interview for the Southern Daily Echo. '… so anything like this tower would be an excellent idea.'

Another speculative project includes a 'full size laser hologram of the *Titanic* to be projected on a curtain of water at the ship's original berth in the city's Eastern Docks.'

There are also plans for a new Heritage Centre which will tell the story of Southampton's maritime history and especially that of the *Titanic*.

Chapter Nine
A Celebrity Life

Over the years Millvina has met a number of other *Titanic* survivors but since they usually encounter each other at well attended *Titanic* related functions there is never much time to chat:

'We just say, "Hello, how are you?" And that's usually the end of it because there are always so many photographers and people who want interviews and autographs. When I first went to America I hardly had time to eat or drink. I was completely surrounded all the time. All us survivors were kept busy so I hardly got to know them at all!'

However, there was one survivor, Edith Haisman, who Millvina did get to know and like over the years by virtue of the fact that they both attended the annual British Titanic Conventions in Southampton:

'Edith was a lovely lady, very sweet tempered. For a while she was the oldest survivor and I was the youngest. She was 15 when the *Titanic* sank and she remembered it quite well. In 1996 I attended her 100th birthday party and was able to give her a big birthday kiss. What an amazing lady she was!'

Although at the American reunions the survivors were usually ushered from one interview or photo opportunity to the next, Millvina did get the chance to spend a bit of time with survivor Louise Kink Pope. Louise had been a child of four years old in 1912:

'I called her "Kinky"! She was a delightful woman, very small in stature but jolly company. We went for dinner together and chatted and laughed away for most of the meal. Not, as you might suppose, about the *Titanic*, but about all manner of things unrelated to the ship.'

Millvina also got to know fellow British survivor Eva Hart reasonably well, but their approach to *Titanic* events could be quite different:

'Eva had been a Justice of the Peace before she retired and was quite an outspoken critic about the recovery of artefacts and altogether a rather formidable lady. She would sign autographs but once she had had enough, that was it - finished! However, she was a very effective public speaker and her speeches were always well received because aside from anything else she could remember the *Titanic* quite vividly. She had been seven at the time and, like me, had lost her father. Whenever I was asked to deliver any kind of formal speech I would make it as informal as possible - much more chatty and friendly. As I've often maintained, I'm not a professional public speaker and never have been - though I've now had plenty of experience!'

Millvina and Edith. Greenwich 1994.

Some *Titanic* related events can be quite stressful. Millvina does not mind taking part in documentaries about the *Titanic* disaster but finds watching motion pictures depicting the tragedy very unpleasant. She remembers one particularly upsetting experience:

'Many years ago I went to see A Night to Remember. I saw it with four or five other survivors in Boston and we all hated it because our fathers had been killed on the ship. It was a dreadful experience. We were absolutely appalled. One person said she had nightmares for weeks afterwards and I agreed that we should never have been taken to see it. I don't want to see anything like that again and even though I've been invited to a few private screenings of James Cameron's *Titanic*, I always refuse. I would not mind the first part, but when the ship is sinking I would be wondering what my father was doing. Even though I didn't know him it would be very emotional. Watching those terrible scenes re-enacted would be too awful for words.'

She has, however, been a special guest at a number of amateur theatrical presentations and plays about the *Titanic* and these she finds far more palatable and genuine:

'I've been getting telephone calls about the new

American *Titanic* musical,' she wrote in 1995, 'which is supposedly costing millions… As I told the callers, I've no idea what to say as I don't know anything about the project, but, if the play is going to be anything like the Wildern School, Hedge End, Southampton one [a local school nearby] then it will be in excellent taste and very entertaining.'

In 2004 the aforementioned *Titanic* musical came to England where it was given its premier in an amateur production at the Gordon Craig Theatre in Stevenage, Hertfordshire. Millvina was duly invited to see it for herself:

'I sat through the first half which was well acted.' she said. 'The players portrayed all the real life characters perfectly and the packed audience seemed to love it. For the second half - which of course included the sinking - I sat in the foyer and signed autographs.'

Live music (particularly classical) has always been a joy to her and on her 90th birthday Millvina invited a small group of family and friends to a hotel in the New Forest to celebrate:

'I love music and luckily my hotel friends knew of a small orchestra so a violinist, cellist and pianist played lovely music for us all the evening. We had a really splendid time.'

Since she also likes the company of children, an invitation to Salisbury Cathedral School in 2004 was gratefully accepted:

'I spent a very enjoyable morning there. The children are all, of course, very musical, and we heard the flute, violin and piano all played beautifully, and the choir sang one or two songs composed by one of their teachers. It was quite enchanting.'

In 1995 Millvina was invited to attend a rather grand *Titanic* function. The *Titanic* Historical Society had decided to hold their annual convention aboard the legendary ship, the *Queen Mary*.

Built in 1936 and considered the pride of the Cunard line for over thirty years, the RMS *Queen Mary* was for a few years the largest

ship in the world. An Art Deco masterpiece renowned for its speed and high quality service, it had an illustrious career ferrying the rich and famous back and forth across the Atlantic.

During the Second World War the *Queen Mary* also saw active war service as a troop transport carrying thousands of men and women in the forces around the world. After the war year she continued her regular service across the Atlantic and in the 1960s had a second brief career as a cruise ship. However, age eventually caught up with her and she was sold in 1969 to the City of Long Beach, California, where she remains moored to this day as a unique tourist attraction and hotel.

Since much of her 1930's charm was maintained, the ship remains something of a time capsule reflecting the glamour of the days when 'getting there was half the fun'!

Millvina found her stay aboard the *Queen Mary* most enjoyable, if a little disorientating:

'It's a wonderful ship of course, quite something and so beautiful inside. However, I must admit that I got lost more than once trying to find my stateroom! There seemed to miles and miles of endless corridors to negotiate. Really, it was quite exhausting!'

The visit threw up other opportunities for sightseeing which included a high speed cruise to Santa Catalina Island, 26 miles off the coast and a tour of Hollywood's most famous landmarks.

In January, 2004, Millvina was invited on the maiden voyage of the new Cunard liner, the *Queen Mary 2* but sadly, much to her regret she had to decline

The Cunard liner *Queen Mary*. Cunard merged with the White Star Line during the period of the building of this ship in the late 1920s.

because said she would have found the walking too much for her.

1997 was a particularly memorable year for Millvina. She was asked by the Titanic Historical Society if she would like to complete her journey to Kansas which the *Titanic* disaster had stalled in 1912. A delighted Millvina accepted straight away and wrote this letter to the British Titanic Society describing the trip:

'In August Bruno and I travelled on the *QE2* to New York with a party of Titanic Historical Society people on their Heritage Tour, a wonderful experience indeed. It was my first Atlantic crossing by ship since 1912.

The trip lasted five days. I wished it could have gone for weeks!' Barbara Magruda of the American based Titanic Historical Society was also onboard and recalls:

'Having Millvina Dean and Bruno, her travelling companion along was an extra treat. They are both so warm and friendly - a real pleasure to travel with. Millvina's endless enthusiasm for life and her incredible ability to remember names, and keep us all straight, continually amazes me. She never seems to tire, despite all the activity around her - her spirits, energy and sense of humour remain constant.'

During the crossing Millvina took part in a *Titanic* question and answer session in the Grand Lounge alongside *Titanic* historian, Don Lynch who would later be an advisor on James Cameron's block buster film, *Titanic*. She was also invited onto the bridge and given the opportunity to push the button to activate the ship's horn at noon.

'We flew from New York to Kansas where we stayed with one of our friends. Soon after getting there I visited the house which had been our family's destination way back in 1912. It was quite exciting seeing the house where I could have lived but for the *Titanic* disaster.

Of course, the media paid plenty of attention to my visit and we did lots of TV, radio and newspaper interviews - it all makes for a very busy and exciting life.'

On arriving at the front door of 3659 Harrison Street, Kansas, Millvina was met by the present owners of the house and a descendant of her great uncle Alfred. Thom Norbury, who is Alfred Norbury's great grandson, greeted her by saying, 'Nice to see you at last!'. The Associated Press picked up the story and articles appeared throughout the world.

'The present owners of the house, Matt and Katie Levi, were charming.' Millvina remembers. 'They even had a glass of champagne waiting for me! I was taken all over the house with a TV crew and saw the nursery which I would have had if things had worked

3659 Harrison Street, Kansas, the intended destination of the Dean family in 1912.

out differently. That was quite an experience I must say.

One of my relatives was at the house waiting to see me, and then I went to a farm about 65 miles away in Prescott where there were eight or nine more. They gave us a lovely all-home-made meal.'

Michael Rudd of the Titanic Historical Society was there to see the reunion: 'It was wonderful to watch Millvina and her family all smiling in animated conversation as they talked about Aunt Gladys, or the Lights, some of whom had emigrated to Canada, or vague recollections of Grandpa Alfred and his wife, Grandma Sarah.'

During this trip Millvina also had the opportunity to visit another ship with a tragic past. The steamboat *Arabia*, built in 1853, had sunk into the mud off the Missouri River in 1856. When the river changed course the mud became a corn field and the *Arabia* lay undiscovered and forgotten for 132 years. In 1985 it was excavated with much of its cargo still intact. Today it is a remarkable museum and time capsule of the Victorian era - rather like touring a department store of the 1850s. Millvina found it fascinating and took a keen interest in all the artefacts which include clothing, plates, medical supplies, hardware, Indian beads and two prefabricated houses.

'We loved Kansas,' said Millvina when she got home. 'Everyone was so nice and I had so many things given to me. The mayor presented me with a handsome book about Kansas, and a pretty hand-painted tile to hang up. He was a darling.'

There was no resting on her laurels either when she returned to England:

'Back home for a rest? I don't think so! Several TV interviews have been arranged and so many people want to come and visit. I have never been so busy in my life!'

In 2002 Millvina was happy to be guest of honour to open a fete celebrating the Bicentenary of her old school. Founded in 1901, the Gregg School had moved from its old location in Cumberland Place in 1948 and was now situated in Townhill Park House, Southampton, a Grade II listed mansion which, coincidentally, was built in 1912, for Louis Montagu, second Baron Swaythling. The gardens had originally been created by Gertrude Jekyll - one of England's most influential Victorian garden designers:

Gregg School where Millvina attended.

'I had to cut the ribbon and 100 balloons floated into the air. It was a beautiful sunny day; there were lots of stalls etc. and a band playing, and I'm sure all the children, their parents and visitors had a marvellous time. I signed a lot of autographs but enjoyed it immensely. I asked the teacher if any of my former school friends would be attending. "Hardly!" she replied with a chuckle.'

Anyone who ever visits Millvina will have the added pleasure of wending their way through the pastoral beauty of the New Forest. This area of Hampshire is mercifully free of overdevelopment and still retains much of its old world charm with its unique landscape of ancient and ornamental woodland.

William the Conqueror created the New Forest around 1080 as his own private deer hunting park. King Rufus was murdered there in very mysterious circumstances in 1100 and the 'Rufus Stone' commemorates the event. These days the area attracts thousands of tourists every year and has become a well loved holiday destination. Covering an area of roughly 1,600 acres it is very popular with campers, walkers, cyclists and horse riders, and has recently been designated as a national park.

Strangers entering the New Forest for the first time are usually surprised to find ponies roaming quite freely within the leafy glades and quiet roads. In fact, an agreement with the Crown settled many hundreds of years ago means that the local farmers or 'Commoners' have the right to graze their ponies, cattle and donkeys without restrictions! Millvina recalls: 'My Grandfather had Commoners rights, and I remember once he let his pigs out to eat the acorns (pannage) and when he returned later to get them they had found their way home before him!

My mother was raised in the New Forest in Bartley and returned there after the *Titanic* disaster. I lived there until I was eight and attended Copythorne School with Vere. When the teacher tried to separate me from Vere, I made such a fuss that they let me go into his class, even though he was a year older. I then returned to Bartley after the Second World War.' She adores the flora and fauna to be found there and likes nothing more than visiting her local pub The Gamekeeper, with her many friends.

Bartley is situated within the parish of Netley Marsh on the western borders of Southampton and the New Forest. Architecturally, there is not a great deal of interest to see there except for a rather pretty Georgian house, now a hotel, which probably dates from the 16th Century when it was a hunting lodge, a Victorian cricket pitch and a church which looks as though it has been constructed from tin!

Known affectionately by locals as the 'Tin Cathedral' the church was built in 1900 and was designed to be not only a place of worship but also a meeting room for parish business. However, by the mid 1990s the building was in desperate need of restoration and a

Millvina and Bruno having a quiet drink in the Royal Oak pub, New Forest.

campaign was begun to save it. Millvina wholeheartedly supported the appeal and in an interview for the Southern Daily Echo she said:

'My mother went to Bartley Church every Sunday and I used to go occasionally. It's a landmark and always has been. People catching the bus to this part of the Forest used to tell the bus driver to stop at the tin church and he always knew where they meant. Often he'd make a joke of it and refer to it as Bartley Cathedral!'

The church was saved from demolition after villagers bought the building for £10,000 and drew up proposals to convert it into a community centre. With financial help from grants of £75,000 the project went ahead and work proceeded at a steady pace. By the end of 1999 the building had been fully restored - just in time for its centenary and the new Millennium. The stained glass windows at the back of the church were dedicated to Millvina's Aunt Gladys – Ettie's younger sister. A delighted Millvina said, 'I'm so glad, I would have hated it to have been pulled down.'

Apart from meeting people and entertaining guests for high tea at her home, Millvina's interests include

The 'tin' church, Bartley, following restoration.

An early photograph of the church at Bartley.

gardening, and watching Coronation Street. She also has a love of cuckoo clocks and has amassed quite a collection. Any visitor who stays for tea will be treated to a veritable chorus of sing-song chirrups and chimes every half hour. Another of her passions is football.

'The World Cup is so exciting for me,' she says. 'I follow all the matches avidly and am glued to the television for hours!'

Even Titanic related trips abroad can throw up some

opportunities to watch the odd match or two such as one to Europe in 2002:

'A short time ago Bruno and I were in Lewisburg (near Stuttgart) for the Swiss Convention. We met all our old, and some new, friends and had a marvelous time. We even watched the Germany v Brazil football match in a German home. The owners were wonderful; they hadn't met any of us before and allowed five foreigners to descend on them. It was because I, a football fan, said I'd love to see the match, that the son of the house, a charming young man, invited us to his home. It was a pity that Germany did not win, not that anybody cared. Football is not one of their interests!'

Millvina has family in Canada and it has always been a special place for her with many happy associations. The Titanic has often been her passport to seeing far more of the country than she would ever have done otherwise. It has also meant she has been treated to some entertaining spectacles. In 1994 she wrote:

'I have just returned from a very enjoyable three week trip to Canada. I was invited over by the Space and Science Centre in Edmonton for the premier of the IMAX film Titanica. My American driver told us that he and Dr. Ballard tried to find the Loch Ness Monster. Being unsuccessful, they then went looking for the

Titanic and you can see the result in the film.

On the opening night I was quite overwhelmed to have a vintage car pick me up, the red carpet was laid down and a Scottish piper piped me into the Space Centre.

[Later during the trip] I said I would love to see an Indian dance. I was invited to an Indian school where some of the children dressed in their native costumes and danced just for me.

I found all the Indians quite charming. I admired a very colourful poster on one of their walls and they immediately took it down and presented it to me!

Visit to the REMP training Academy Regina, Saskatchewan 1999.

They also gave me a small carved wolf. The wolf, I think, has something to do with the spirit of their ancestors. I was then presented with some plaited grass called 'sweet grass' which, when lit at one end, filled the air with its scent…'

She returned again in 1999:

'I visited various cousins, one in a quite isolated area of Saskatchewan who breeds buffalo and wild boar. I kept well away from those! The second day we were there, two bears visited my other cousin's farm just half a mile away. My cousin said, "Oh, that happens. They're just passing through!"'

Whilst in Edmonton she was able to catch up with some old friends at a rather special meeting:

'I was invited to an Indian Pow Wow. I've always been fascinated by the Canadian Indians and so I was delighted to go. There were tribes there from everywhere, all in handmade, wonderful, exotic clothes - and the noise! And you think discos are loud! - but I have never had such a lovely time. I love colour, so this was magic.

I have a number of Indian friends, and I did not know that I was going to be called upon to speak to all the assembled tribes. I didn't mind. I made my little speech and then shook hands with the elders, lots of them, and had a most beautiful day.'

In April, 2003, Millvina received a letter from a young couple who had a very personal request. Would it be possible, they wondered tentatively, if they could name their new baby daughter after her? Millvina was surprised and flattered at such a tribute and gave her blessing.

The Southern Daily Echo ran the story:

Millvina, meet our own little Millvina!

A young couple were so inspired by the story of the youngest survivor of the *Titanic* disaster that they have named their baby after her.

Sanya and Adam Ward were delighted to come to Southampton to meet the original Millvina… and introduce her to little Millvina.

Sanya, 31, a training manager from Aldershot, said: 'My husband Adam has always been interested in the *Titanic*. It stems back to his great-grandfather who used to go past the docks every morning and saw someone painting a picture of the ship.

He asked for first refusal on the painting and bought it. Adam always saw the picture hanging up when he was young and he eventually inherited it.

He mainly collects books about the *Titanic* and was in seventh heaven when the film came out because there were so many new ones to collect.

When we found out I was pregnant we knew we wanted to choose an unusual name and because of Adam's interest in the *Titanic* we decided on Millvina.'

'…It's really flattering to have a baby named after me [said Millvina]. A Close has been named after me but this is the first time a baby has been given my name so it's quite an honour.

I've no idea where my parents got my name from. The closest anyone has ever come to having my name was a little girl who went to the same Red Indian school as me in Canada but she was called Mellvina.'

Baby Millvina, nicknamed "Milly" by her parents, is causing quite a stir with her unusual name. Her mother said: 'People have been surprised by the name because most of them have never heard it before but everyone has said that they think it's a lovely name.'

Sidney Sedunary who lost his father in the disaster, Millvina and Mary South who lost her Grandfather, outside Southampton maritime Museum.

Into the 21st Century

Millvina has remained happy and single all her life. When asked, at the age of 95, why this was so, she said simply: 'I never married because one man wasn't enough. I loved them all!'

How does she like being a 'celebrity'? She laughs at the idea. 'I only hope people don't think I'm big headed.' she adds with a chuckle.

She loves meeting new people. This, she admits, has always been one of the best aspects of being a *Titanic* survivor. She takes an avid interest in her friend's lives and

Millvina in the midst of yet another interview - this time in the Scottish city of Dundee.

her legendary hospitality is a talking point among those with an interest in the *Titanic*. Had she not been on the *Titanic* in 1912, she probably would not have enjoyed the rich tapestry of experiences she has had in her latter years, but one can be sure she would still

Millvina and Bruno in Dundee with their hosts, after having visited the HM *Frigate Unicorn*, the oldest British-built warship still afloat at the Victoria Dock. One of only six ships still surviving, that were built before 1850 anywhere in the world.

have been the same kind, considerate and sociable lady she is today. This extract from one of her letters demonstrates her characteristic sense of spontaneity and fun:

'I can't remember if I told you in my last letter that I was put up as a prize in a charity auction! What will they think of next? Anyhow, the gentleman who "won" me came from London with his daughter, and my friend, who arranged it all, came with her daughter, and brought sandwiches, tarts, cakes, etc. and we all had a lovely picnic.'

Millvina never seems to mind being asked about the *Titanic* - even though she has told her story many, many times. The following anecdote by Brian Ticehurst, one of the founder members of the British Titanic Society, demonstrates the extraordinary effect she can have on new audiences:

'It was 1995. At that time I was Newsletter Editor of the British Titanic Society's Newsletter and also organiser of the yearly Convention, and as usual it was being held at the Southampton Hilton Hotel at Chilworth on the outskirts of the city.

About a week before the Convention a teacher at a private school in London (who was a member of the BTS) phoned me to ask if it would be OK to bring two coach loads of children in to see the *Titanic* exhibition on the Saturday afternoon? - I agreed on the condition that there would be enough adults to control the children.

The children were en route from London to the West Country for the start of a weeks Camping holiday and the subject of the *Titanic* was part of their curriculum.

Came the day the two coaches arrived with approximately 100 children and staff and they filed quietly into the hotel and started to look around - the whole weekend was a complete sell out and the whole place was very crowded.

Unbeknown to me, Millvina Dean had been doing one of her 'walkabouts' and was approached and asked if it was possible that she could say a few words to the children and of course she agreed.

Millvina and Bruno with their distinguished hosts in Dundee, among them the Lord provost, and Dowager Countess of Strathmore.

The first thing I knew about it was when I was summoned by the management of the hotel to help them sort out a problem - the problem being that one of the passageways running alongside the main Exhibition Room to all the Fire Exits was completely blocked.   When we arrived it was to behold a sight that I shall long remember.

At the far end of the passage was Millvina with Bruno.   Standing alongside her and in front of them sat, on the carpeted floor of the passage,   all the schoolchildren. Along the walls and at the back it was packed with adults all listening to her (there must have been over 200 people in that passage) - you could have heard a pin drop.

Millvina was giving a very witty account of what had happened to her at some of the *Titanic* related events that she had been invited to in this country and abroad and the kids and the whole of her audience were lapping up every word of it. When she had finished there was a very lively question and answer session with a lot more laughs.

While this was going on I looked at the manager and under manager who had summoned me to sort it out and I noted that they were both listening to every word and were as enthralled as everyone else.

So I just stood there and said nothing.

A few minutes later it was all over and most of the people dispersed except the usual crowd gathering around Millvina for a signature or a quick word with her.

The managerial people came back to earth also and I was then given a lecture on Health and Safety regulations and told of some of the many rules that had been broken etc., I just smiled and apologised. They would never have believed me if I had told them that I had known nothing about it!

It was such a magical spontaneous event and one I am sure a lot of those children will never forget.'

Today, Millvina lives in a New Forest Nursing Home where she has been since breaking her hip in the Autumn of 2006.   Her road to recovery has been a long one, due to her contracting a hospital 'superbug,' but her fighting spirit emerged and Millvina has battled her way back to health. Unfortunately the long recovery process has meant that although her mental faculties are as sharp as ever, she is now confined to a wheel chair. Her adaptability to the situation has been admirable: 'What can't be cured, must be endured,' she says cheerfully. And her life carries on busier than before.

She spends her days seeing visitors from all over the world, signing cards, writing letters, and conducting interviews. Weather permitting she likes nothing better than to be taken out, either to her cottage, close by, sitting in the garden watching the birds, or enjoying a pub lunch down the road at The Gamekeeper. She lives each day in the present, and keeps up to date with what is going on in the world, as well as taking an interest in the lives of the nursing home staff. She knows all their names, ages, countries of origin, and marital status. In fact, she often knows more about them than they do about each other!

Millvina's new residential status has meant taking stock of the past. During the summer of 2008 she decided it was time to re-evaluate some of her possessions – particularly those with a *Titanic* link. One of these was a rather battered old suitcase which, so her mother told her many years ago, had been given to her in New York directly after the disaster. Also unearthed were papers relating to the Dean's stay in St Luke's hospital and a letters relating to the Titanic Relief Fund - all of great interest to Titanic historians and collectors. After a great deal of thought Millvina offered up these items – along with some other *Titanic* related ephemera – for auction. Funds raised would go towards her care home bill. However, her decision whipped up a storm of dramatic media headlines:

'TITANIC TRAGEDY TOUCHES HEARTS'
read one,

'FORCED TO SELL TITANIC MEMORIES'
cried another. The *Daily Mail* had this to report:

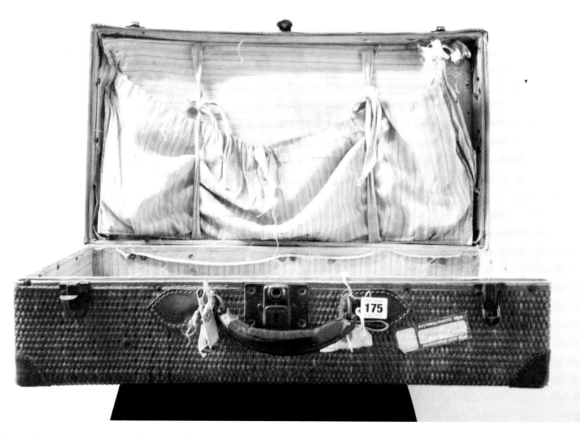

The suitcase at the centre of the world's press in October 2008. *Courtesy of Henry Aldridge & Son, auctioneers.*

Last remaining survivor of *Titanic* forced to sell souvenirs to pay for nursing home fees

The last remaining survivor of the *Titanic* is selling mementoes of the liner to pay for nursing home fees.

Millvina Dean hopes to raise more than £3,000 from auctioning off the *Titanic*-related items.

The 96-year-old needs the money to pay for fees at the nursing home where she has lived for two years.

Millvina Dean: The last remaining survivor of the *Titanic* is having to sell her treasured mementoes to pay for nursing home fees

She is also auctioning off rare prints of the *Titanic* that have been signed by the artists along with compensation letters sent to her mother from the Titanic Relief Fund.

Miss Dean, from Southampton, Hants, was a two-month-old baby at the time of the 1912 disaster and is the last person in the world to have survived it who is alive today.

She has been living in a private nursing home in the New Forest since having a hip operation two years ago and now needs to raise money to carry on staying there.

Miss Dean said: 'I was hoping to be here for two weeks after breaking my hip but I developed an infection and have been here for two years. I am not able to live in my home anymore.

'I am selling it all now because I have to pay these nursing home fees and am selling anything that I think might fetch some money.'

Mrs Dean was given the wicker suitcase and its contents by the people of New York as they had lost all their possessions and money in the sinking.

Miss Dean, a spinster, said: 'The case was given to my mother when we were in New York and she brought it back with us.

'It wasn't in too bad a condition and I used to take it away on holidays with me.

'When the wreck of *Titanic* was found 20 years ago I was invited to conventions all over the world and I took it with me then.'

Andrew Aldridge, of Henry Aldridge and Son auctioneers of Devizes, Wilts, said: 'The suitcase is a very emotive and unusual item and epitomizes what the people of New York did for the *Titanic* survivors. It also highlights what state the survivors were in

when they got to New York. Many people lost everything down to the clothes they were standing in.'

Thus, it seems that even at the venerable age of 96, Millvina and the *Titanic* are still news!

Millvina's tireless energy and patience in dealing with such a familiar subject is commendable, her manner always gracious and humble. She recognises that as long as there are people with a feeling for the past, a love of history and an interest in the human condition, the legend of the *Titanic* will live on forever.

'I often wonder what my life would have been like if I had not sailed on the *Titanic*,' Millvina wrote some years ago. 'I can only speculate. Possibly, instead of being an ordinary English citizen leading a very uneventful life (apart from living through two world wars) I would have been an ordinary American citizen.

The *Titanic* will never die. It has a mystique about it which fascinates people. We learn from the fate of this beautiful ship that 'Man proposes but God disposes.'

The beginning and the end of the story. Milvina is seen with Vere when she was just a few weeks old.

Acknowledgements

A very special thanks must go to Millvina Dean whose reminiscences have formed the basis of this biography. Brian Ticehurst, co-founder of the British Titanic Society was of invaluable help in checking facts. John Lawrence for photography, Alastair Arnott, Dawn Squire, Elsie Mayo and Barbara Farquaharson for helping with the Dean family research and supply of images. Anthony Cunningham would like to mention his dear friend Leza Mitchell who has been the best companion during long car journeys down to the New Forest, and his mum and dad for their unwavering support and love. Sheila Jemima would like to dedicate it to her children Clare and David.

Bibliography

Books: Boyd-Smith, Jan and Peter Southampton: Gateway to England (Red Post Books 2000)
Butler, Daniel Allen Unsinkable: The Full Story of the RMS Titanic (Da Capo Press 2002)
Cunningham, Anthony The Titanic Diaries   (Silver Link Publications Ltd 2005)
Goldsmith, Frank J. W. Echoes in the Night (Titanic Historical Society 1991)
Hyslop, Donald, Forsyth, Alistair and Jemima, Sheila Titanic Voices Memories from the Fateful Voyage (Sutton Publishing 1998)Hutchinson, Gillian The Wreck of the Titanic (National Maritime Museum 1994)
McCarthy, Pete The Road to McCarthy (Hodder and Stoughton 2002)
'The Branscombe Lace-Makers' edited by Barbara Farquharson and Joan Doern 2002

Journals: The Atlantic Daily Bulletin, Journal of the British Titanic Society: PO Box 401, Hope Carr Way, Leigh, Lancashire, WN7 3WW
The Titanic Commutator, The official journal of the Titanic Historic Society, Inc: 208 Main Street, Indian Orchard, Massachusetts, USA.

Newspapers: The Southern Daily Echo, Newspaper House, Test Lane, Redbridge, Southampton, SO16 9JX

Websites: Branscombe: www.branscombecountrycottage.co.uk
Cobh: www.cobhmuseum.com
Cobh (Titanic connections): www.ttrn.com/grassrootscolleenfliednercobhire
Dulwich: www.southwark.gov.uk/DiscoverSouthwark/HistoricSouthwark/Historic
VillagesSection/HistDulwichHistory.html
Encyclopedia Titanica: www.encyclopedia-titanica.org
Gregg School: www.gregg-school.co.uk/about/about_us.asp
Honiton Lace History:www.honitonlace.com/honitonlace
New Forest: www.newforesttrust.org.uk/thenewforest.asp
Princess Victoria cruise ship: www.simplonpc.co.uk
Southampton and Titanic sites: www.bbc.co.uk/southampton/features/titanic/tour.shtml
Tin Church, Bartley: www.hants.org.uk/bartleytinchurch/publicity.htm